Cruising Florida

CRUISING FLORIDA

by Red Marston

Ziff-Davis Publishing Company
New York

Some of the material in this book has previously appeared in *Boating* magazine.

Manufactured in the United States of America.
First printing, 1981.
Library of Congress Catalog Card Number:
81-51352
ISBN 0-87165-100-9
Ziff-Davis Publishing Company
One Park Avenue
New York, N.Y. 10016

To Peggy, loyal wife, severest critic, and peerless navigator of *Final Edition*, who has always told me where to go—afloat and ashore—with unerring accuracy.

CONTENTS

PREFACE

It's ironic that, for a state that has been so well publicized, no full-length book has been devoted to cruising all of Florida.

Magazine and newspaper features have picked away at the cruising theme for years, but mainly in four-color, picture-postcard versions of the good life afloat in Florida; the net effect has been like nibbling away at the hors d'oeuvres while passing up the dinner.

Thousands of boat owners in Florida and countless others who visit by boat don't know the state's huge cruising potential. The cruising treasure that is Florida's is not entirely obvious when viewed merely through the coastline and shoreline that appear on the map—the lengths of which dwarf those of all the other mainland states in the country.

For one thing, and most obvious, most of Florida is an immense peninsula, automatically assuring that this weather-blessed state can show at least two attractive coastal faces.

West of the peninsula's upper section is another cruising area known as the Florida Panhandle, a large area never fully appreciated. It has miles of sparsely populated beaches on barrier islands, wide, long bays and uncrowded sounds—almost a "last frontier."

This is a book about cruisable Florida, written from the narrative as well as reportorial approach, perhaps taking up where guide books leave off.

While my wife, Peggy, and I frequently appear on the pages as we share our observations, impressions and (sometimes) hard-won knowledge, tell about interesting places and people off the more popular cruising paths, we make it a point not to simply dredge details from the ship's log in order to move us from port to port, anchorage to anchorage.

There is some risk in writing extensively about cruising because it means different things to different people. What impresses one, depresses another. The mere act of moving from Point A to Point B satisfies many. Exploring for good restaurants along the waterways excites some to the same extent rowing ashore and landing on an unpopulated barrier island stimulates others. There are those who want to get-with-it, others who want to get-away-from-it.

Our Florida cruising has been done largely on *Final Edition*, a 38-foot trawler that draws three and one-half feet, powered by a single diesel engine that has propelled us well over 34,000 nautical miles, ranging from Texas to Maine.

We wrote for both sailboats and powerboats, keeping in mind that people had to be able to *get* to to the places being written about. Our thinking was that in Florida four feet of draft is a good average, three and one-half better, and five feet the outer limit for gunkholing.

We wrote more about the lesser known places about which little is published, such as the Gulf of Mexico. And because we know that many who cruise have considerable curiosity about their surroundings, we have included stories of unusual people and a little salting of history in the book.

We hope you will have a feeling of kinship for the French lady with her fiefdom in Indiantown; for Darwin, the Hermit; even for Emperor Ed Watson, the notorious killer from Chokoloskee in the Florida Everglades. You will meet the spinster Warren sisters of LaBelle, sitting out their years on a once-famous yacht that is now deteriorating in a lagoon just off the Okeechobee Waterway, and Milton the Cop, in Apalachicola. You'll hear the story of how the Panhandle city of St. Joseph was destroyed by yellow fever, hurricanes and fire, a series of calamities that gave evangelists cause to cry out that it was God's punishment for a wicked community. We tell of meeting Bette Davis up in Shark River in the Everglades; recall the June day in 1942 when four Nazi spies landed from a German U-boat near Jacksonville Beach, and of cruising down Condominia Canyon on the Florida east coast on the Intracoastal Waterway.

We offer, of course, cruising guidance, matters of navigational and piloting information woven into the chapters as *Final Edition* moved along both coasts, across the state, down the Florida Keys to the Dry Tortugas. The mission, from the outset, was to entertain as well as inform.

We would like to acknowledge our thanks to Dr. Paul Minthorn of Tampa, a trawler owner and cruising buff, for his insistence this book be written before it was too late—too late for whom he did not say; to Barbra Somerville who did the typing and was kind enough to say she enjoyed doing so; to the St. Petersburg *Times* for the use of its clipping files. And, finally, to Peggy. The dedication of this book to her does not begin to reflect the enormous amount of time she spent reading copy, editing, counseling, intercepting telephone calls, researching, and putting up with my haggling over words and tenses.

FOREWORD

Born a Yankee, Red Marston has been a dedicated Floridian for the past 30 years. In *Final Edition*, his 38' custom trawler yacht, he has cruised Florida as has, perhaps, no other yachtsman, gunkholing along the Panhandle waterway, poking his nose into backwater ports, observing—and participating in—the life of the locals. This book, although not a cruising guide in the strict sense, is a highly personal and very complete discussion of the entire state of Florida, from the cruising yachtsman's point of view.

Red began his long career in journalism as a reporter for the *Boston Herald*, moved on to sports writing for radio, then in the early 1950s joined the *St. Petersburg Times* as outdoor editor. Cruising Florida in his 36' lobster boat *Sea Scribe*, and later in *Final Edition*, he became a spokesman for the yachting fraternity, both in the pages of the newspaper and through his many articles in national marine magazines. When he noticed that several boats and lives had been lost in the long offshore passage in the Gulf between Apalachicola and Clearwater, he began a campaign to get the Coast Guard to place lighted markers along the so-called Big Bend route, a somewhat longer course that follows the bend of the land and allows access to two ports of refuge. His campaign was successful when, in 1974, the Coast Guard installed the markers.

Another of his crusades concentrated on the issue of bridges over various Florida waterways that were closed to pleasure-boat navigation during periods of peak vehicular traffic. His position on this issue has always been a reasonable one, but his newspaper columns and magazine articles have, for years, called public attention to new regulations that effectively block navigation of the waterways for several hours each day. It's safe to speculate that more bridges might be closed more hours but for his efforts.

It is unquestionably true that Florida's bays, lakes, rivers, sounds, islands, waterways, port cities and climate make the state a cruising ground without equal. Red and Peggy Marston have spent decades confirming that proposition, and this book is the happy result.

The practical information is here: how to meet and pass tugs and barges in the narrow waterways; where to anchor, or not to anchor, in innumerable ports; how to anticipate, and if necessary cope with, a hurricane; even where to get a diesel engine repaired. More than that, though, is the sense of being in close communication with a seasoned cruising man, a man who is truly interested in wildlife, the beauties of nature, the personalities of the people encountered along the way, local history, and—particularly—where the best seafood may be found.

It will be hard for most people to read this book without beginning to plan an extended Florida cruise.

Dick Rath
Editorial Director
Yachting Magazine

BELOW FLORIDA'S EYE IN THE SKY

Chapter 1

Once every nine days, one of the magic eyes in the sky—the Landsat satellite, 570 miles up—passes in orbit over Florida. In a period of 111 seconds it scans all 58,560 square miles of the state. In that brief, intense examination, Landsat looks down on the finest year-round, weather-blessed cruising grounds in the United States.

The satellite is concerned with the big picture but the information it transmits back to earth makes clear that no other state has—is surrounded by—so much cruisable water, or has such an intricate interlocking of waterways, including one that crosses Florida all the way from the Gulf of Mexico to the Atlantic Ocean. Even the habitually hard-to-please type should be able to find a pleasant cruising niche—maybe several—with 1,350 miles of coastline to choose from. Only Alaska has more, but that state has seasonal limitations. California's amiable relationship with the Pacific is confined to only 850 miles of coastline.

Florida, with a meandering shoreline of about 8,500 miles, abounds with casual cruising opportunities. It has many bays, sounds, rivers, creeks, bayous, navigable swamps, countless islands, major ports and, incredible in this age, many miles of uncrowded beaches, some of them reachable only by boat.

I picture Florida's shape as a holstered, long-handled pistol, with the trigger guard located near Apalachicola, at the eastern end of northwest Florida. Landsat, with its capacity for exquisite detail, reinforces the image in our mind's eye. The satellite picture emphasizes, above all else, that Florida is a classic peninsula, a shapely, fortuitous geological occurrence dating back to the Ice Age.

The picture shows a Florida whose surface skin is covered with pockmarks, indicating the presence of over 7,000 lakes. Each has a name and at least 10 acres of surface water. The long-fingered, tiny, crooked cracks in the picture are rivers. Thirty-seven of them are 25 or more miles in length. Many of them are part of a state network of designated canoe trails. At 270 miles, the St. Johns River is the most cruisable and extensive of all, but for practical cruising purposes, the marked channel distance, from the Atlantic to inland Sanford, is 157 statute miles.

Good reason, then, for the claim that about 80 percent of the people live within six miles of the water, with most concentrated along the two coasts in four or five general areas. If you visited only those spots, you could not be blamed for envisioning Florida as being ringed by one continuous seawall behind which people are jammed in a vertical world of high-rise structures called condominiums.

But the state has not been entirely blind to the lure of its water, its weather and the trend to "people-stacking" along the coast. The state

is gamely waging a counter-offensive by buying considerable shorefront property in the more isolated or less populated sectors—not an easy proposition in a state that has been a developers' and real estate paradise for well over 100 years. Much has been done, however, to head off the black-topping of saltwater marshes and estuaries to make way for supermarkets and shopping centers. The ospreys still have a chance.

The Five Pieces of Florida

Trying to cruise all Florida in a single journey would be difficult and impractical. The distance could be covered within a calendar year, but it would be a race rather than a cruise.

I think of cruisable Florida as five parts. They are: the Florida Panhandle—Big Bend to Cedar Key; from Cedar Key down the west coast to the Gulf side of Everglades National Park; the Florida Keys; the cross-state Okeechobee Waterway; and the Florida east coast.

There is a certain unevenness about the Florida cruising scene. Much is known about some places, little about others. Northwest Florida is forgotten territory as far as cruising is concerned. It could be that it is too distant from the large concentration of boats in south Florida, or even from the much closer, heavily boat-populated Tampa Bay.

The area is more seasonal than southern Florida; winter cruising is limited. Limited, too, are marine facilities here compared to other parts of the state. The Big Bend area intimidates the less adventurous. The Panhandle is far from boatless but is still a "foreign" land to thousands of central and south Florida boat owners.

For those who want to be away from crowds, who like a reasonable challenge in their cruising range, who are able to be self-sufficient for two or three days at a time, the Florida Panhandle is the place to go.

The distance from Cedar Key to the far end of Everglades National Park is roughly 200 nautical miles. Within this area is what is generally considered to be the Florida west coast. Tampa Bay, through Sarasota, is the central core of it.

The Florida Keys are to some extent upstaged by the glamor of the Bahamas, but the Keys have attributes that have long endured and brought pleasure to countless cruisers. Key West, for example, with its colorful range of heritage, is a city with a lifestyle that defies imitation; the Dry Tortugas chain boasts a fort that stands 65 miles out to sea.

That the Keys are too shallow for cruising does not stand up to close examination. We tell of our Keys cruise of over 400 miles to prove that it is both pleasant and practical to do so. This string of islands stretches well over 100 miles out from the tip of Florida.

You can also cruise across the middle of Florida, from coast to coast, using the Okeechobee Waterway between Fort Myers Beach on the Gulf of Mexico and Stuart on the Atlantic. It's a 151-mile journey across the state that provides a look at another, inner, dimension of Florida. The trip calls for a casual navigation of two canals, a beautiful river, crossing a world-famous lake, and passing through five easy-to-cope-with locks. It's a trip through citrus, cattle, farming and sugar cane country, a cruise that deserves to be made for its own merits rather than just as an expedient way to get from one coast to the other. In an average year, about 6,000 pleasure and commercial boats travel the waterway between Stuart and the west coast.

Good cruising territory is not man-made. It evolves through land mass changes along the coast or inland.

Florida received more than its fair share of good cruising areas, the west coast in particular. This side of the state offers the most varied cruising for both power and sail boats. Its bounty includes two large combination bays and harbors, and miles of beaches and barrier islands which can be cruised on either side.

The centerpiece of the area is Pine Island Sound, a 21-mile-long body of water that is an unspoiled treasure by modern standards. It is convenient to large boat centers, yet far enough for prolonged stays or weekending.

Between Tarpon Springs and Fort Myers Beach a full round of cruising is available, with opportunities for swimming, shelling, clamming, diving, beach-walking and good fishing.

On down the west coast, beyond Naples and Marco, the mangrove coast dominates, revealing an entirely different aspect of Florida. The Gulf of Mexico, depending upon its mood, either strokes or pounds the land perimeters for the 200-mile distance.

To many, the Florida east coast is the real Florida; the rest of it is over-there-somewhere to the west. The traffic down the Intracoastal Waterway (ICW) from Norfolk to Miami would undoubtedly support that belief. Most of this coast stretches out for 418 statute miles, from Fernandina Beach at the Georgia border to Miami. The first 350 miles for some cruisers merely lead up to the celebrated Gold Coast, a 70-mile spectacular strip of land between Palm Beach and Miami, with Fort Lauderdale in the middle.

In the "season," which is mid-October to mid-May, there are probably more yachts in that 70-mile strip than anywhere else in the

world in a similar distance. If you've seen it, you are inclined to believe it.

Florida east coast cruising has been maligned as much as praised. The Gold Coast is not the Valhalla of the cruising Corinthian, but for thousands that area has more to offer than any other section of Florida.

No one spot is typical of the east coast. The Gold Coast is just one of many features. The satellite sweep would reveal Biscayne Bay and the reef islands to the east, a cruising ground almost in the shadow of Miami; the intimate lushness of the Indian River, just north of Vero Beach, numerous inlets punching holes into the coastline, and the Intracoastal Waterway, a long, narrow Main Street for cruising migrants.

Farther north, the big shoulder of Cape Canaveral pushes its bulk out into the Atlantic, jarring the uniformity of the coastal strip. The St. Johns River, flowing northward more or less parallel to the coast, makes its bid for union with the sea, turning eastward beyond Jacksonville, heading for Mayport.

Thirty miles north, the transition into Georgia is made, with no particular line of demarcation to tell one state from the other.

Florida, on the whole, is not part of any mold, so polished and uniform along its vast perimeters that to cruise on farther is to see only more of the same. Its peninsular shape provides two sides to cruise; two perspectives for myriad cruising tastes.

THE GOOD LIFE AND HURRICANES

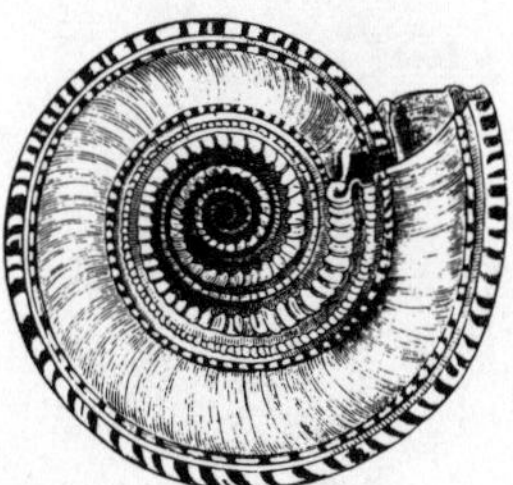

Chapter 2

It helps to understand that Florida is many things to many people. The state is overwhelmingly populated with people from somewhere else. Even those who consider themselves "transplanted Yankees," who arrived early enough to now have children in high school or college, are quick to qualify their current residence—they're always from somewhere else.

The most finely tuned ear will not be able to discern a mother tongue identifiable with Florida, unlike the accents of Maine, Brooklyn, Boston, the midwest or the deep South—immediately identifiable; not so, in Florida.

If there is one tongue that can be considered native to Florida, it is that heard in the rural, upper central and northern tiers of the state. It is spoken by the Florida "Cracker;" but the definition of the "Cracker" is a matter of opinion.

Al Burt, roving columnist for the Miami *Herald*, writes there is a Florida Crackerland, a sort of sub-state. "While it may look like Georgia, and sound like Georgia, sometimes even act like Georgia, it is true Crackerland Florida," reports Burt, adding, "It's southern by culture, Georgian by infiltration and Floridian through enlightenment."

There are Cracker pockets scattered south of Gainesville, but Yankee and Hispanic transfusions strongly dilute their purity, according to Burt. Some say, in jest, that Jacksonville is the largest city in South Georgia. I can't vouch for that, but along the Gulf Coast the fishing villages of Horseshoe Beach and Steinhatchee have a high percentage of Georgia expatriates.

There is more than one Florida. The Gold Coast—Palm Beach-Fort Lauderdale-Miami Beach—lifestyle and political philosophies differ drastically from those of the determined conservative citizens of the Florida Panhandle. It's not so much income differences, more tables of values and priorities.

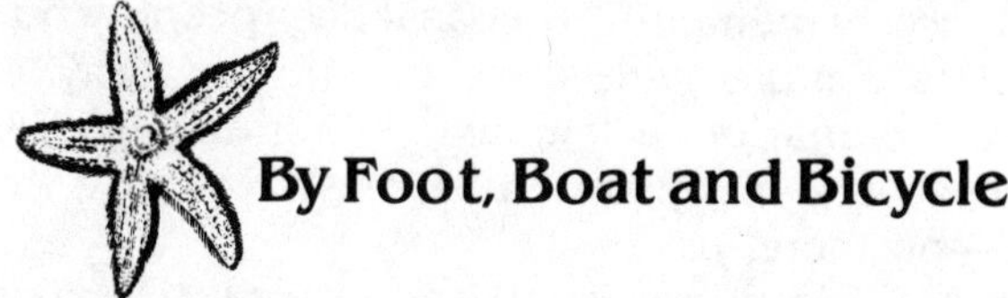

By Foot, Boat and Bicycle

The lure of Florida endures, evidenced in many ways, but none more obvious than the boatman's attraction to it. The drawing power of the good life afloat affects boats used for fishing, sailing, cruising, exploring rivers, racing, water skiing, skin diving and, of course, tooling around in fast runabouts to impress the girls.

Though Florida is thought of almost exclusively as a tourist and

Doug Thatcher, a retired Fort Wayne, Indiana fireman, cruises into St. Andrews Marina, Panama City, bound for Clearwater after a trip down the Mississippi. How do you fit a bicycle, shipshape fashion, into a 14-foot boat? You don't; you hang it out on the port bow and hope for calm waters.
Marston photo

retirement state, it has a fast-growing young to middle-aged population. The national movement south of industrial firms continues, in part because their employees want to live in Florida now, not just retire to it later. A good percentage of this new work force becomes involved with boating—boosting Florida to the half-million boat registration mark.

The fall migration to Florida along the Intracoastal Waterway is a fascinating experience, bringing together as it does people who "dare to be different." It is a mix—some are just running away, others running to a fixed destination, a few just rolling dice against the future. Perhaps those who enjoy the cruise most are those who are fulfilling a dream—no more, no less.

In traveling the Atlantic Intracoastal, and other Intracoastals as well, Peggy and I have met and talked with scores of waterway travelers. We have traded information and mechanical skills, cheered each other on, and listened sympathetically to those whose hopes and plans have come apart, stranding them psychologically if not physically.

Of all the Florida-bound waterway adventurers we have ever met, one that stands out in our recollections was Douglas Thatcher, a retired city fireman from Fort Wayne, Indiana. We were aboard *Final Edition* at St. Andrews Marina, Panama City, when we first saw him, powering into the marina in a 14-foot, low-freeboard aluminum outboard with a bicycle lashed outboard of the portside bow, the wheels just inches above the water. Elevated, fore and aft along the centerline, was a propped-up pole over which a folded tarpaulin was hung.

The boat's operator peered around tentatively, as if looking for a berth. Just ahead of us was a space which the little boat headed for.

The man was in his mid-60s, I judged; his 14-footer was loaded with storage boxes, gasoline containers, camp stove and assorted gear—but our eyes kept straying to that bicyle which, besides looking outlandishly unnautical seemed much too large for such a small boat.

"I'm Douglas Thatcher from Fort Wayne," he introduced himself, and I invited him aboard *Final Edition.*

He told us he had launched the boat at Madison, Indiana, on the Ohio River about 50 miles above Louisville, three weeks before. His destination was Clearwater.

His cruise down the Mississippi had been a refreshing, rewarding experience, because he had met so many thoughtful and kind people, strangers who showed much interest in his experiences.

Sailors who cruise, especially some distance out of their own immediate area, know there is a peripheral zone along the waterfronts that seems to be inhabited by people who welcome new arrivals. Some walk out onto the docks to say hello even before the boat of a stranger is secured for the night. It is not unusual for someone to say, "If you need a car to go shopping, you can use mine." (In Edenton, South Carolina, the owner of a marina once offered us the use of his station wagon for the weekend, explaining he had another car he was taking over to Cape Hatteras where he planned to do some fishing. There hadn't been more than 10 minutes of conversation between us before he made this kind offer.)

Doug Thatcher, we learned, had always liked children and when around them, always had candy to give them. While candy-givers around children are automatically suspect, apparently it was no problem to Thatcher. In small river towns, the sight of his little putt-putt boat with bicycle attached naturally aroused the curiosity of children.

"They'd ask me all kinds of questions, where I had been, where I was from, where I was going and why," Doug told us. "We'd talk for a long time and some said they were going to get a boat when they grew up. I'd pass around candy and we would all talk some more."

While aboard *Final Edition,* talk turned to Thatcher's having to somehow cross the Big Bend, the curved, exposed body of water lying ahead of him. There was no safe way to do it in his little, low-to-the-water 14-footer but perhaps he could skirt along the shoreline. Peggy asked him if he had charts.

"Well, to tell you the truth," he revealed, "I came down the Mississippi just using a road map, but I know I'll have to get some charts here. I want to do things right."

We got out some charts and discussed various routes, but neither Peggy nor I wanted him to attempt the Big Bend by any route. He couldn't have had more than 15 inches of freeboard. His only engine was a 20-horsepower Johnson. Fuel capacity was whatever could be stored in four, five-gallon gasoline cans.

We hoped that by the time he reached Carrabelle, 86 miles from Panama City, he would change his mind about trying to make that last, 150-mile leg to Clearwater. When we got up the next morning, Thatcher had already left.

As the days passed, Peggy and I wondered, and yes, worried about him. Several weeks went by with no word. Finally, one Sunday morning back in our home port, I called the Thatcher home in Fort Wayne.

Doug came on the phone and reported, "Well, like you folks said, it was rough between Apalachicola and Carrabelle. I got soaked. At Carrabelle, I was told it got squally nearly every afternoon. I heard stories about boats getting in trouble out there in the Gulf. I kept looking at those charts your wife marked for me.

"After a couple of days waiting for the weather to clear and trying to decide what to do, I finally figured I'd better quit while I was alive. So I called my son and he came to get me. But I have no regrets. It was a wonderful experience and I will never forget it."

The Florida Hurricanes

Florida has hurricanes just as California has mud slides, forest fires and earthquake tremors, just as gales occasionally pound the coast of Maine and summer squalls rip through Chesapeake Bay. A volcanic mountain in Washington blows its top and a tornado touches down briefly, but disastrously, in Kansas. There is no safe haven. Once that is accepted, it is easier to get on with cruising.

If you want to play percentages with Florida hurricanes, the two months to leave the state are August and September. But there is no guarantee you'll escape a hurricane by sailing off to some other place along the Gulf of Mexico, or hot-footing it up the Atlantic seaboard. Florida hurricanes, though they seldom start here, have been known to wind up in Canada. In 1954 we left Florida for a summer of cruising in New England, only to be pummeled by Hurricane Carol in Marion, Massachusetts, and by Hazel in Chesapeake Bay.

If one were to play the odds, the best place to be in Florida is Jacksonville. But that's just for a given year, not forever. The averages come out that there's only a one-in-50 chance of Jacksonville being hit by a hurricane. If it were our luck to be there when the one-in-50 was about to occur, we'd head inland up the St. Johns River and find any one of a number of good places to ride it out.

Some other odds: one-in-30 at Daytona, one-in-20 at Tampa-St. Petersburg. The statistics slant the other way for Miami and Key West, where chances are reduced to one-in-seven for a given year. Jacksonville, until September 1964, had not experienced a hurricane in nearly eighty years. Until that time it was the only big city on the Atlantic coast from Boston south which never had sustained winds of hurricane force in a tropical cyclone in modern times.

The one advantage the Atlantic coast of Florida has over the Gulf of Mexico side is that storms can, and do, curve northeastward away from land. But once a hurricane enters the Gulf of Mexico, it has to reach land somewhere. The longer it takes for the hurricane to blow ashore, the more intense it becomes, in most instances. Even then, however, weather-wise boat owners overtaken by great storms can make out by taking early evasive action.

Peggy and I have worked out a general plan of operation, but nothing so precisely procedural that it should be considered hurricane gospel. In good measure, it is the sum of much trial and error based on our actual experiences in hurricanes.

When a hurricane starts, we begin listening to tropical weather reports, issued daily. Weather terms such as "tropical waves," "low pressure areas," "bands of heavy showers in the Caribbean" attract our attention. When a disturbance reaches tropical storm status, especially if we are in Florida and the forming action is in the Caribbean, Peggy starts noting the coordinates and tracking the progress of the storm.

Satellite pictures on television support the old axiom that "seein' is believin'." Today, anyone who wants to be informed about a major storm can be. It is not necessary to wait for the newspapers.

Early in the potential hurricane picture, we look at our options—

where we would prefer to be, if possible. Where we would prefer not to be, but might have to be, is something else to think about.

In planning our 1975 trip from Tampa Bay to Brownsville, Texas, and return, there was considerable family research on occurrences of hurricanes along the Gulf coast on a month-by-month basis. From that study, we made the decision to start as early as possible in May.

We had a hurricane-free cruise, but we were back home only a couple of weeks when, in mid-September, Hurricane Eloise came up the Gulf and hit the Florida Panhandle we had so recently passed through. Ducking hurricanes can't be planned even by the best of research efforts but the percentages are worth trying. Backed up by a bit of luck, things may turn out fine.

Peggy and I, well before the inevitable which is sometimes too late, proceed on the assumption that an approaching hurricane could reach us. There can be profit in such pessimism. If the storm doesn't reach us, so much the better; the homework, the preparation, is not all lost time. The discipline of it all is worth something, and worthwhile if it has to be used some other time.

Hurricanes that arise when one is cruising strange territory add extra pressure to the situation but the planning basics remain generally the same. Some of them:

■ Get away from other boats. A crowded harbor taught us that. Avoid keeping a boat at a dock or tied to pilings. Study charts for possible hurricane "holes" and protected areas. Study the type of shoreline—is it rocky, marshy with mudbanks, trees with limbs hanging over the water, ringed with a seawall? How good is the holding ground for anchors? Pick a good spot, get there early. If it is a good one, you'll soon have company—local boats may already be there. Determine the swinging room.

■ Try to obtain as much early local knowledge as you can but realize that in the end you'll have to make your own decisions. Check the supply of batteries. Be sure fuel and water tanks are topped off, that there is extra food in the refrigerator or ice box. Have the chafing gear ready to put on.

■ Lower the Bimini top on the flying bridge, if you have one; lash it securely. Stow loose gear. Secure halyards. Study the predicted tides, allow for a sizeable buildup of tidal water and adjust anchor scope accordingly. Be ready to cope with a heavy rainfall. Break out the old towels. The wind will force rainwater into places you would not believe possible.

■ Determine what should be done with the dinghy. In Hurricane Carol we left it in the water astern, let it almost fill with rainwater. It helped cut down tacking around on the mooring. Eventually, in both

Hurricanes Carol and Hazel, we had to turn it loose, but not before tying an old life jacket onto the painter. Both times we retrieved the dinghy after the hurricane passed.

The transient cruising skipper shouldn't count much on Florida marinas accepting his business when a hurricane is coming on. On the east coast, in particular, some of the big ones, such as Pier 66 in Fort Lauderdale, have a firm rule that all boats must leave the marina. But some marinas, in less exposed areas, do take in boats that are not regular customers. One, in North Palm Beach, guarantees a berth, but a fee for that option is charged on the lease agreement during the hurricane months. Some sailors regard this extra fee as another form of insurance.

It seems to us that those cruising when a hurricane threatens have a few choices denied the local resident, who must divide his time between home, family, business and, perhaps, a boat also. Cruisers can plan with a little more deliberation.

Where are the best places to ride out a hurricane in Florida? No one can realistically assemble a list of foolproof places. But personally, I'd prefer to be somewhere on the Caloosahatchee River east of Fort Myers. Only trouble with that is, too many people also feel the same way.

If I were in the Florida Keys, I'd head for Shark River in Everglades National Park and tie up to the mangroves. They can't be pulled out. The boat may be scratched up but the tree limbs have a cushioning effect against the high velocity wind blasts that always come.

Two Winners over Hurricanes

The theory that a boat can survive a hurricane, with or without persons on board, is more than wishful thinking, providing there is good preparation and the companion of the evening is good luck. We shall write of good preparation on the yacht *Virago*, and good luck on the yacht *King Tut*.

Did any boats come through that incredible, ghastly 220 mph Hurricane Camille in 1969, that monster storm that drove vessels ashore along the Mississippi coast and carried homes off their foundations?

Several boats did, in fact, and one that did belonged to an esteemed cruising acquaintance of ours. Not only did Art Terry, of Ocean Springs, Mississippi, ride out Camille, but he stayed aboard his boat

during Hurricane Betsy in 1965 and Frederic in 1979. It might be said that Terry is getting pretty good at riding out hurricanes.

Then there is Bob Strohm of Fort Myers Beach, who twice "lost" his yacht in Hurricane Agnes, class of 1972, in the Dry Tortugas. Each time he got his Grand Banks 33 back in one piece, but in neither instance was Strohm, or anyone else, aboard. Strohm did not just walk off his little yacht. He did leave some instructions for anyone who might find *King Tut*, should she be blown off her mooring at Fort Jefferson on Garden Key.

Terry is a New Orleans-based marine surveyor with considerable commercial and pleasure boat experience. His current yacht is the 40-foot trawler *Virago*, familiar to many a few years back when it was the *Penobscot*, then owned by author-boat builder Carl D. Lane. A picture of her appears on the cover of Lane's book, *Go South Inside*, which is about cruising the Intracoastal Waterway and living aboard boats in Florida.

It is Art Terry's contention that pleasure boats can survive the worst of gales and hurricanes if there is a reasonably protected place to take them, if the defense set up against the storm is practical, and the element of luck is not all bad. An unattended boat that breaks loose and drifts down on one that has been intelligently prepared can trigger a disaster. That is a painful observation since that happened to us once and we subsequently had to tie our craft to the top of a tree.

When the wind and water reversed direction, our boat literally came down a limb at a time. Seamanship normally does not involve forestry but it was important, in saving our boat, which was also our home, that we were aboard to cope with unusual situations.

Art Terry is a strong believer in staying aboard during a hurricane. He does not inflict that preference on others who may not have the stomach for it or have other priority values ashore; for him, it worked—three times in succession.

In Hurricane Camille, his boat was a 40-foot shallow draft powerboat locally referred to as a lugger. Terry, well in advance of the giant storm, took it into a bayou off the Jordan River above Bay St. Louis, Mississippi. He double-anchored it, snugged things down, even secured a well-fendered small sailboat alongside. The eye of Camille passed by less than two miles away. The only damage was a few scuffed areas on the sailboat.

Terry knew the importance of getting behind some sort of protective windshield of land, even buildings. Out in the open Mississippi Sound, Camille was blowing 220 miles per hour. Where Terry's lugger was secured—below a line of trees—the wind velocity on the boat itself may have been reduced to 90 knots. Anchoring in a protected place also proved itself when Terry rode out Hurricane Betsy in the husky lugger.

In Hurricane Frederic, Terry left his Ocean Springs dock and went to a pre-determined anchorage which Terry describes as an "appendage" of Fort Bayou. There he made a four-point mooring, tying off to trees. (Art prefers oaks over pines; they are less likely to be toppled.) He had maneuvered so that *Virago* would be in the lee of the treeline protection, yet safely enough away should any tree fall. The choice of "tree anchors" was made so that *Virago's* bow would be into the wind. She was in 10 to 12 feet of water. Art's choice of an anchorage was hardly solitary. About 35 other boats, many of them fishing craft, also were in the general area. The brunt of Hurricane Frederic was borne by Dauphin Island and Mobile, 40 miles east of Biloxi, but it was strong enough where *Virago* was to more than justify the seeking of shelter.

Circumstances were considerably different when Bob Strohm found himself out in the Dry Tortugas, 65 miles west of Key West, with Hurricane Agnes bearing down on him. Bob and his wife, Connie, were there as part of a cruising group called the Calloosahatchee Marching and Chowder Club based at Fort Myers Beach.

King Tut was anchored off Garden Key. Agnes moved along so fast it was too late for most of the cruising boats to leave, but a shrimp boat, bound for Fort Myers, took aboard some of the club members, beating the storm back but not by much.

Others accepted the invitation of the Fort Jefferson park rangers to retreat to the brick fort. Food and water were brought from boats and pooled. There was a supply of extra mattresses at the fort, but otherwise the rangers had accommodations and supplies sufficient only for normal staff usage.

All the boat skippers had prepared their boats as best they knew how, within the limits of their equipment. Strohm's Grand Banks 33 was in about seven feet of water, riding to two anchors, one a Danforth 22-pounder, the other a small Navy anchor. On the Danforth, he had 300 feet of line to work with; on the Navy, much less. Strohm told us, when we met him later at Cabbage Key in Pine Island Sound, that he hadn't been happy with his ground tackle setup but that it was all he had.

Aboard *King Tut*, he did some interesting things in the way of preparedness, notably, make signs, taped and displayed prominently in the cabin. They read, in large lettering, "This is not an abandoned boat." His reasoning was that if *King Tut* broke loose, he didn't want her finders to think they had come upon some derelict or that his

trawler had been abandoned in the face of the oncoming hurricane.

Other preparation included disconnecting the batteries, stowing all small items, shutting down the sea cocks and lashing heavy gear in the cabin. But he forgot one thing: removing the contents of the refrigerator; the unit itself he had secured firmly.

Bob Strohm and Connie thought a lot of *King Tut.* According to papers aboard, it was hull No. 1 of the Grand Banks 33-footers built in Taiwan. Around two o'clock in the afternoon, a small boat came out from the fort and Bob left *King Tut.*

It was a miserable night at the fort. The rains came. The wind howled. A crisis was avoided narrowly when someone was caught trying to raid the rationed supply of cigarettes. The overriding concern for most, however, was how their boats were making out in the anchorage. In the darkness and driving rain, it was impossible to see them.

In the first few minutes of daylight, Strohm was up to check on *King Tut.* She was missing! So were two sailboats. Park rangers radioed the small Coast Guard unit at Loggerhead Key Lighthouse, not quite three miles away. Would they please see if they could see the missing yachts?

From the 151-foot-high tower, a lookout saw all three boats on Brilliant Shoal, two miles or so north of Loggerhead. It was determined, by taking bearings, the boats were not drifting. Anchors now appeared to be holding.

Strohm, the skippers of the sailboats and a small group of volunteers went out in a small boat but the water was so rough, especially around Brilliant Shoal, that it was deemed unwise to try to swim to them. Seas were running high, though the wind had dropped to about 35 mph.

The disappointed rescue party went back to the fort and spent another fretful night. At first light, the men at the lighthouse focused their binoculars on Brilliant Shoal. The sailboats were still there—but *King Tut* was nowhere to be seen.

Strohm had a right to feel depressed. First *King Tut* was lost, then found. Now, gone again. He had second thoughts; he wished he had tried to swim to her when she was on the shoal. The rangers put through another call, to the Coast Guard at Key West.

A day later, while still pacing around Fort Jefferson, Strohm was notified by radio that *King Tut* had been found. The Coast Guard, searching for another missing boat, had come across her well to the northwest of Loggerhead and had towed her to Key West.

Strohm hitch-hiked a ride to Key West on a boat that had safely ridden out the storm at Garden Key. Bob boarded his boat and made a quick inspection. Despite both anchor lines having been wrapped in chafing gear, they had chafed through.

Inside, the signs were still in place. The cocktail table had broken loose but everything else appeared in order. The refrigerator had not moved.

Strohm opened the door and peered inside to find that Hurricane Agnes had mixed him a giant salad of everything that was in breakable containers, including ketchup, mustard and a sprinkling of olives atop an otherwise unidentifiable combination.

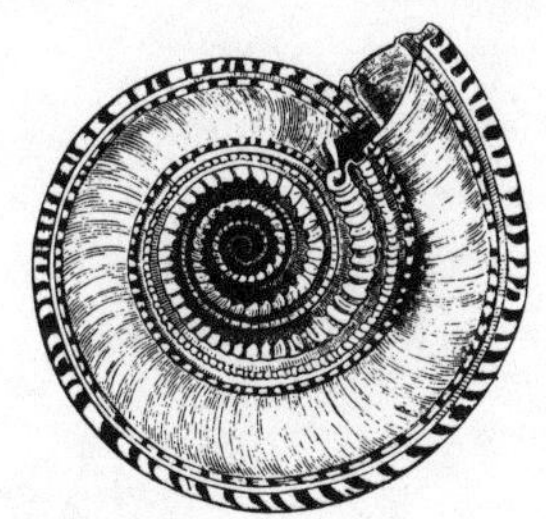

UNDERSTANDING THE GULF

Chapter 3

The Gulf of Mexico, with 582,100 square miles of water, is the largest gulf in the world. It is also the ninth largest body of water.

The Gulf of Mexico washes onto the shores of five of our states for a combined coastline total of 1,631 miles. Florida, with 770 miles of it, has almost twice as much as Louisiana, the second beneficiary. Texas is third; Alabama and Mississippi barely get a taste of the Gulf's salt.

The Gulf also exerts tremendous influence on tiers of states well removed from those contiguous to its waters. It deserves to be better understood. It is a cousin of the world famous Gulf Stream; as such, it is sometimes regarded as playing a secondary role.

Many times in the course of a year, its weather system alone is a presence felt far north and east of the Rio Grande. One can be sailing, as we have, in far-off Maine in weather directly related to warm moisture coming all the way up from the Gulf. In the winter, a Great Lakes blizzard may have received much of its energy from warmer air that originated in the Gulf of Mexico.

The physical makeup of the Gulf is unique, if for no other reason than that it is a catch basin for 40 percent of the nation's water drainage. Oceanographer Dr. Carl Oppenheimer estimates that it receives water from a two-and-a-half million square mile area, from the Appalachian Mountain chain on the east to the Rocky Mountains on the west, excluding one small area around the Great Lakes.

The Gulf of Mexico is host to water from the Mississippi, Ohio, Illinois, Wabash, Cumberland, Rio Grande and other rivers and streams. The huge basin not only accepts their flow, but also that of spring-fed streams along the Florida west coast that pour millions of gallons into it.

The U.S. Geological Survey figure for the overall discharge into the Gulf is well over 550,000 cubic feet of water every second of every day.

The expanse of the Gulf is deceiving. So nearly surrounded by land, it would seem difficult to get lost in it; one can, but it doesn't last forever. Turn right or turn left, you've got to get to shore somewhere.

A few years ago, before Loran (long range navigation) equipment became standard on fishing vessels, we picked up a call, on our radio, to a shrimp boat captain out of Tampa who was nearing the Gulf of Mexico's Bay of Campeche shrimping grounds. Then, it was permissible to fish there.

"Hey, Joe," the Tampa captain was asked by another shrimper, apparently uncertain as to his own whereabouts, "where you at now?"

"You gotta chart, Sam?"

"Course I got one, whaddya think."

"Okay, Sam, where I'm at is right under the G in the Gulf of Mexico."

The Gulf is the working world of the big guys—tankers, freighters, large fishing vessels, special craft allied with the oil industry, ocean-going tugs, barges and, among others, the sizable fleet of shrimp boats working the Florida and Texas sides of it.

Most cruising boats work their way around the Gulf shoreline rather than taking offshore routes. A few sailboats, however, headed for a Florida winter or the offshore racing circuit, will depart Galveston or Biloxi and cut time and distance by heading across to Clearwater or Tampa Bay.

Even in cruising, there are occasions when circumstances dictate speeding up the schedule. But we rarely go offshore on time-saving missions. We understand the limitations of our trawler yacht and even better, how much we are willing to put up with physically. The one great luxury of retirement cruising is not to have to be somewhere at a definite time, and to be in the position to wait out bad weather.

The Profile is Low

The *U.S. Coast Pilot* describes the Gulf of Mexico coastline from Key West to the Rio Grande as low and generally sandy. It is not the type of coastal terrain that provides good charted landfall features. From Anclote Key, off Tarpon Springs, to St. James Island on the west side of Apalachee Bay the coast is low and marshy, with the shoreline broken occasionally by creeks and rivers. Inland a mile or two there are pine forests. From St. James to the Alabama line, as seen from the Gulf of Mexico, the coast is a mix of barrier beaches, low, wooded sand islands, ideal for those who are comfortable cruising to and around them.

Between Clearwater and Naples, however, the west coast skyline has changed drastically over the years. Starting in the early 1960s, a few condominiums began to appear along the beaches, but as 1970 started the condo boom was in high gear. Some of the old landmarks disappeared behind high-rises or were knocked down and cleared away to make more room.

"Condominium" navigating is practiced to some extent in Florida, not building by building, but by using those that have relationship to passes, or in some way are clues to identifying a city. Water towers, more often seen on the east coast than on the west, are on the charts, but today's navigators probably are happier when the towers display the name of the community in bold letters.

Local Gulf coast fishermen, who used to count on a cabbage palm near a point of land or maybe a cluster of pines for returning landfalls, now have a wide choice of structures and a pick of colors for return guidance after an offshore trip.

The only mangrove coast that exists now on Florida's west coast is that area below Marco Island, a dozen miles south of Naples. Marco, once the haven of snook, redfish and tarpon fishermen, was densely populated with mangroves. Today it is a famous resort and a retirement community. There is a 500-room, 10 story-high hotel and a nearby airstrip. Near the south end of the island another development has 18-story-high buildings overlooking Caxambas Pass.

The buildings make impressive landfalls for anyone cruising up the coast from Shark River or Cape Sable. Those farther offshore and heading north can use them for identifying the island. Be sure the course line clears the Cape Romano shoals off the south end of Marco Island.

Most boats, west-coast-bound from the Florida Keys, head across Florida Bay towards Cape Sable on the southwest tip of the Florida mainland. Others, departing Key West, may elect to head over the long-haul course, 118 miles to the lighthouse on Sanibel Island at the entrance to San Carlos Bay.

A variation on heading for the west coast out of Key West is to set a course to Cape Romano, a distance of 78 miles. It would be prudent for those not familiar with Cape Romano to time arrival there in the daytime to cope with the shoals.

Bank Blink and Flash of Green

A sense of awareness, natural or developed, adds to the enjoyment of cruising. Children, and adults for that matter, can be introduced simply to it in Florida waters by raising the question whether mullet, so often seen jumping out of the water, always land on their left sides. Another attention-getter is to claim that nine out of 10 times a flight of pelicans will be odd-numbered.

Sooner or later, almost surely, someone will ask, why do the mullet jump? The common explanation, including the one heard from some marine scientists, is that they jump for the sheer fun of it. I have

watched them under water and seen them, for no apparent reason and not being chased by anything, suddenly speed up to the surface at an angle—and jump. It is not uncommon to see them make a series of three or four jumps.

Those who are more attentive, those hoping to see the unusual, will be interested in two phenomena that may be observed along the Florida west coast.

One is called bank blink; the other, the flash of green.

On bright, clear days, cruising along the coast where the sand is white, a reflected, white light may be seen. It will appear hanging over sand banks or dunes. Our first encounter with it raised speculation that a minor dust storm was causing it. But the steadiness of the light persisted for several minutes as we closed the distance. We were observing what is called bank blink.

It is, simply, reflected light from the sand and can be seen from a considerable distance. It is said to appear only in the tropics and then only under ideal conditions. One of the best places to observe it is along the Florida Panhandle beaches, especially between Destin and Panama City where the sand is exceptionally white and powdery.

The flash of green, also called the green flash, is a real meteorological phenomenon according to *Sea Secrets*, published by the International Oceanographic Foundation at Virginia Key, Miami. It states: "The large refraction of celestial light sources near the horizon that produces it is associated with a relatively large prismatic dispersion. This dispersion causes the last segment of the setting sun or planet to appear green for a few seconds.

"The green flash is seen only on very clear days, usually over the ocean. If the atmosphere is both abnormally clear and abnormally refractive, a blue flash can be seen. In rare cases, a continuous spectral color change from yellow through green to blue is possible. The same phenomenon can be observed at sunrise but in reverse order."

One has to be looking almost directly at the sunset to see the flash of green. I have seen it only once, though I never miss a Gulf sunset while cruising. The sun was just touching the horizon when the flash came. It was an instant flash. I cried out to Peggy who was next to me and though she quickly turned, it was too late to see that electric moment. It may be that on a day the bank blink can be seen, atmospheric conditions for the green flash are also favorable.

The Gulf Loop Current

Each spring a warm, wonderful gift from the Caribbean comes to the Gulf of Mexico. It is called the Loop Current, a strong flow of deep blue water that surges up from the Caribbean in the spring and sweeps past the Yucatan Peninsula into the Gulf. There it makes a loop, first in a broad northwest-to-northeast arc, then down the Florida west coast.

The current, sometimes 100 miles wide, other times much less than that due to wind and atmospheric conditions, appears off South Pass in the Mississippi delta, then circles past Pensacola, Destin and Panama City Beach before dropping down the coast 80 to 100 miles offshore.

Although the loop functions mainly from early spring through fall, it is believed to be present in other months, but to a greatly reduced degree. It begins each winter with a buildup of water in the Caribbean from currents that meet there. Driven by winds and related forces, in March the water streams through the gap between the Yucatan Peninsula and Cuba, most of it going through the Straits of Florida and eventually up the east coast.

But the Loop Current breaks off and enters the Gulf. Subtropical seas go through decided changes as the waters warm. Currents often grow stronger. The mixing of cold and warm waters alters the chemistry of seawater, producing plant and animal life that attract food-foraging fish.

Riding the current as it begins its move toward the Mississippi delta are marlin, sailfish and various species of tuna. Broadbill swordfish were first thought to be Loop Current hitch-hikers, but since they are caught commercially in winter months it is possible their migration in and out of the Gulf is not related.

The existence of the Loop Current was suspected in the late 1940s and 1950s, then confirmed in the 1960s. It opened up a new frontier of gamefishing which brought renewed economic life to the Florida Panhandle; large charterboat fleets now operate about seven months of the year, with the largest fleet based at Destin.

The current is affected by three major influences in the north and northeast Gulf: the Mississippi delta, the De Soto Canyon and the continental shelf. The shelf is an extension of the continental mass into the ocean. Material scrubbed from the land by wind and water erosion has been deposited in the Gulf, forming the shelf. Centuries

of wave action have gradually shaped a gentle, sloping floor that extends under water 10 to 100 miles out.

The delta provides a good source of minerals and life-sustaining nourishment for plants and minute marine animals so important in the sea's life cycle. The De Soto Canyon is a tremendous depression in the Gulf of Mexico, south of Pensacola and west of Cape San Blas.

The canyon drops from 283 fathoms to 448 fathoms in a relatively short distance. Farther southwest, it gets much deeper than that. The east side of the canyon is about 60 miles southwest of Destin. It still is a long run for charterboats out of Pensacola, Destin and Panama City, but some are set up for two- and three-day stays. Today, the fuel factor is at least equal to the expenditure of time.

Geologists may have varying theories about the origin of the canyon, but there is no doubt that the fishing is good there. One scientific explanation is that colder sub-surface waters are pushed against the Canyon's steep walls. This produces an upwelling of plankton and other nutrients that, as always, attract small fish followed by large fish.

Other than the phenomenon of the Loop Current, the Gulf of Mexico currents are generally weak in the open Gulf and minimal along the coast, presenting no problem of consequence to those who cruise.

Weather satellites have removed many of the mysteries of current flow and direction, but occasionally a bottle with a note in it will be found and stir public interest again. One such incident involved the Gulf in 1969.

A drifting bottle with a message inside washed ashore at Fort Myers Beach. Seven years earlier, in 1962, a member of an Explorer Scout group had tossed the bottle into the Atlantic Ocean at Wassaw Island, Georgia. Where did it go in the intervening years?

One possible route was a ride up the Gulf Stream where, near the stream's approach to Europe, the bottle was carried along the edge of the Canary Current on to the South Equatorial Current system off Africa, thence into the Caribbean. From there, it almost had to go through the Yucatan Channel into the Gulf of Mexico. Whether eddies of the Loop Current, or perhaps strong winds, deflected the bottle toward Fort Myers Beach or it made the full loop trip is not certain.

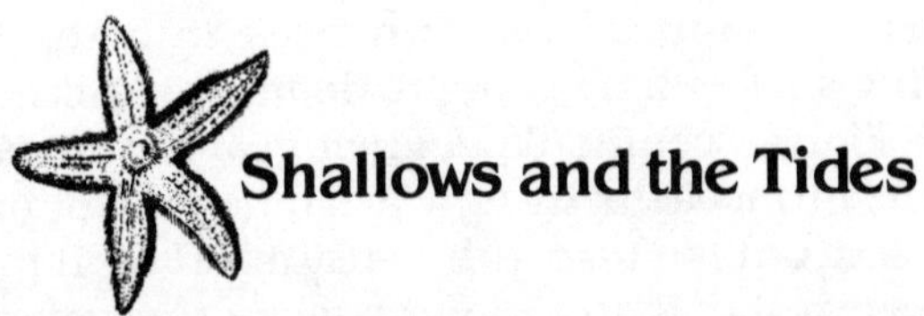

Shallows and the Tides

Those who arrive in Florida to cruise, fish or live on the west coast often express surprise at the generally shoal water and the fluctuations in the flooding and ebbing of the tides.

From Cedar Key to on past Naples, longtime coastal fishermen subscribe to the popular consensus that "the Gulf bottom drops about one foot per mile westward." That satisfies the casually curious. The National Ocean Survey (NOS) charts show the contrary, however, though not dramatically so in the first few miles.

One has to travel 15 miles due west of the mouth of Tampa Bay's Egmont Key to reach 60 feet of water. Another 40 miles offshore brings 120 feet of water. The 100-fathom curve is reached at about the 100-mile distance from Egmont. The broader picture of the Gulf depths, between the Dry Tortugas and Cape St. George at the east end of the Florida Panhandle, shows the 10-fathom curve varying from 10 to 40 miles offshore and the 100-fathom curve varying from 90 to 140 miles.

Depths change considerably between Cape San Blas and the broad bight of land sweeping around to the passes of the Mississippi. In that sector, the 100-fathom curve is only 30 to 60 miles out, but off St. Andrews Bay at Panama City, depths of 60 feet are reached close to shore.

The shallow water that concerns small boat owners and cruising yacht skippers runs close to shore. From Apalachicola all the way down to the Florida Keys, eight to 10 feet is common in many cruising areas.

Even moving offshore a bit, putting the low-lying land just below the horizon, between Steinhatchee and Cedar Key, 18 feet of water is considered a lot. The depth is 10 feet or less on a course from Cedar Key to the Anclote Keys.

No boat should be without a depth indicator when cruising Florida's west coast. We find it more than a handy reference; Peggy employs it as an essential tool for navigating the miles of shallow water cruising.

I have been asked frequently about practical drafts for boats, particularly sailboats, for use on the Florida west coast. Three to four feet of draft is fine, a "go most anywhere" draft. Five feet can be carried many places; six means mainly using the Gulf and routinely

using only the deeper channels that run back into the bays. A cruising boat drawing six feet isn't going to do much gunkholing on the west side of the Florida peninsula. A great deal of moving about will be done along the Intracoastal Waterway. The project or intended depth is set at nine feet but isn't a depth to rely on. Make it more like seven, somewhat less in the winter months when the water can be dropped by northerly winds.

The absence of two sets of tides per day (two floods, two ebbs) puzzles the Gulf newcomer if he has ever lived in a part of the country where tides are part of daily life. Dr. F. G. Walton Smith, in his book *The Seas in Motion*, refers to the Gulf's seeming tidal inconsistencies compared to other waterfronts.

He writes: "The weak tides of the Gulf of Mexico do not exceed two and one-half feet. Because of its dimensions, the Gulf is only in weak resonance to the tidal rhythms, responding to the diurnal tides but scarcely at all to the semidiurnal tide. As a result the Gulf tides are diurnal everywhere except on the west coast of Florida."

Tides that rise and fall once daily are diurnal. Semidiurnal tides are two complete sets of tides, common along the Atlantic Ocean. (Neap tides, often referred to by fishermen as "nip" tides, occur between the periods of spring tides with a smaller range and weaker flow.)

Notes Dr. Smith, "The tides appear to oscillate with the tides of the Straits of Florida, which sweep around the Gulf. Tidal variations are governed by the extremes of lunar declination rather than by the phase of the moon. A similar situation exists in the Caribbean."

Douglas McVicar, writing in *Sail* magazine, noted: "The tidal pattern on each place on the coast is as unique as a man's fingerprint. No other place can have exactly the same combination of tide-determining factors: shape of the shoreline, location and size of river outlets, cleanness of water, latitude and longitude and shape of the sea floor."

That the Gulf of Mexico has its own style and rhythm cannot be denied. It cannot be dismissed as a mere cousin of the Gulf Stream.

PLEASURES OF THE PANHANDLE

Chapter 4

It has been observed that the southerner has a tendency to keep private his natural luxuries and thus discourage visitors. That could be one of the reasons the Florida Panhandle, the northwest region stretching roughly from Apalachicola to Pensacola, is not as well known as it should be to those who cruise.

Few in the Panhandle have ever encouraged us to write about the charm of their favorite places. They don't seem to mind general complimentary remarks, acknowledging that a certain town is particularly friendly, that the fishing, hunting and oystering is good. They do mind, however, superlatives being laid on some specific place or places dear to them, their personal preserves of pleasures. We have, on occasion, been lightheartedly implored to "lay off" writing about some particular place because "it will only bring people who will spoil it," or, "Hey, don't write about that anchorage; that's where we go on weekends!" Provincial protectionism, under the circumstances, is understandable.

The Panhandle is a huge area to cruise in, really more than enough to go around without crowding. It is one of the least populated areas in all Florida. The beaches along the Gulf of Mexico, some of them of a quality and beauty not surpassed elsewhere in the nation, extend for miles. Yet, despite concentrations in a few summer tourist communities, the beaches are largely uncrowded, almost deserted in many places.

Along the beaches, state and federal money has been used for parks and refuges.

Lumbering is a big industry here, and the Panhandle isn't going to be overrun by the masses in the foreseeable future unless the big, powerful lumber companies decide to go out of business. In some counties, they own a large percentage of all the heavily forested land, behind the waterfront where the seafood industry thrives.

The fall of the year—good most anywhere, to be sure—finds northwest Florida at its best. The air is crisp and clear. The threat of hurricanes is gone. Oystering picks up. Fish shake off the lethargies of the summer's warm water. The beaches, with the tourists gone, are virtually abandoned. Lucky are those who can manage a cruising schedule that puts them between Fort Walton Beach and Cape San Blas in the fall, still leaving time to head south before the winter winds pick up.

The Panhandle has the "seasons" which so many northerners who move to Florida say they miss most. In northwest Florida there is a winter, but not so much that anyone has to shovel it. The hunting season is anticipated. Many who think of Florida as being barren of game just haven't checked out that part of the state.

We like the variety this part of Florida has to offer the cruiser. Behind the crescent-shaped beach line, the dazzling dunes and wooded islands, are bays through which threads the Gulf Intracoastal Waterway. Passes lead in and out, Gulf-to-bay, 20 to 60 miles apart.

At Apalachicola, going west, the waterway ducks inland, through woods, between sandy cliffs, across lakes and bays, past marshlands that create the sense of protection one feels in much of the Okeechobee Waterway.

Cruising northwest Florida is enhanced if one is aware of just a little bit of the history of the area. It is easy to think of Florida from Tampa Bay southward as being the center of development, but during the early days of the state, development was concentrated in the upper reaches. One year after the United States acquired Florida, in 1821, Pensacola was selected as the site of the organizational meeting of the Legislative Council. Later, when cotton was king, Apalachicola was one of the great ports in the country. Fleets of vessels anchored in Apalachicola Bay waiting for dock space in the city.

Apalachicola was hardly a buttoned-up community either, having its share of ladies of the evening, saloons and gamblers, plus all the tawdry trappings of a booming seaport. Unlike its neighbor, St. Joseph, Apalachicola survived its outbreak of yellow fever, the hurricanes did less damage and it recovered from a series of fires. Old Apalachicola continued on.

Pensacola

If Pensacola now seems remote from the more popular Florida cruising areas, it was much more so for a small group of East Floridians who attempted to sail to it for the Legislative Council meeting scheduled for June 10, 1822.

In 1822, people from St. Augustine could travel to Pensacola by two routes—by land through the unsettled wilderness or on the often-stormy seas. Under the most favorable conditions, the land journey took a man on horseback several weeks.

The four delegates sailed from St. Augustine on the sloop *Lady Washington*, departing May 30. After experiencing calms and squalls, *Lady Washington* put into Matanzas, Cuba, on June 22, to renew her supplies of food, water and wood. She was then 12 days late for the meeting and almost a month overdue when she arrrived off Pensacola on July 7.

Because of heavy seas, the sloop with the tardy legislators aboard was not able to enter the port of Pensacola, and eventually capsized. The passengers and crew clung to the sides.

The four representatives from St. Augustine did eventually arrive in Pensacola, late, exhausted, but alive. They fared better than a colleague who took a different vessel from St. Augustine and perished in a storm. The council was organized with only eight of its 13 members present, but then there was another problem. An epidemic of yellow fever broke out in Pensacola. The council wisely retreated inland to an area known as Cantonment to finish its founding work.

No such struggle faces the Florida-bound cruising contingent that arrives in Pensacola each fall. They come down the Mississippi River, or from ports in Alabama, Mississippi, Louisiana and Texas. The distance from Pensacola to Miami, via the Okeechobee Waterway, is about 750 statute miles, nearly twice as long as from Fernandina Beach, at the Georgia border, down the east coast to the same destination.

For a city that has much appeal, particularly from an historical standpoint, Pensacola has a shortage of transient marina space, particularly in the summer months when the resort facilities are busiest.

Pensacola Bay is 12 miles long and tends to stretch out the hunt for space. But it is a beautiful bay, with nearby beaches and a well marked, deep pass into the Gulf. Day sails, beach parties, visits to historical places and good restaurants make a stay worthwhile.

There are many places to anchor. We have spent pleasant hours in five-mile-long Big Lagoon, west of Pensacola. The Gulf Intracoastal goes through it, and it's ideal for stopping short of Pensacola in the afternoon, putting you in a good position to move on to that city the next day. Our cruising friends in the Big Lagoon area report it was badly damaged by Hurricane Frederic in 1979, but it has recovered with the enterprise and determination that waterfronters seem to be able to summon in the wake of a disaster.

The entrance to Pensacola from the Gulf is as spectacular as one will see on the Florida west coast. The Pensacola Light towers 191 feet above the water and is set back on the north shore of the entrance. Across the pass to the east is Fort Pickens, a favorite of the history-minded. The entrance to the pass is 110 miles west of Cape San Blas, a direct line distance. The contour route along the beaches is farther, though more interesting.

Bayou Chico, four miles northeastward from the ICW, is the nearest marina point to the city. This is the place to be for shopping, boat repairs or an overnight berth. The hospitable Pensacola Yacht Club, one of the nicest in the South, is available to members of accredited clubs, though it, too, has a space problem.

One of the most frequently raised questions along the cruising front is, "Where's a good place to eat?" I often have felt the impulse to say, "On my own boat," which is a tribute to Peggy and meant as such. But that comment could be mistaken as being rude. We generally plead ignorant to the where-to-eat quandry but, like most others who cruise, there are some small special places we like and return to.

Peggy and I appreciate hearing from those who know of a place that is particularly good, perhaps easily overlooked by those cruising along. It was lady skipper Lynn Noble, of Fort Walton Beach, who urged us to dine at the Coppersmith's Galley in a Pensacola complex known as the Seville Quarter, in the heart of the historical district. The Quarter is graced with gas lamps that once lit the streets of Birmingham, England.

We had a memorable luncheon, served family style, as we sat in spindlebacked chairs from an old monastery, with stained glass in the skylights overhead. The galley deck is of two-inch, solid heart pine over 100 years old. The wall panels came from solid cypress doors. The all-oak doors and brass hardware came from World War II Liberty ships.

For the opposite in atmosphere in the Quarter, there is Rosie O'Grady's, a saloon built in Pensacola's old 1871 Commercial Hotel. Rose's is the place to be if you like strumming banjos, Dixieland bands, vaudeville, minstrel acts, dancing waiters and silent movies. Then there's a World War I aviator's pub called Lili Marlene's, a gathering place for old aviation buffs and the present-day Navy fliers from the Pensacola base.

The Seville Quarter is more than a good place to eat; it is a place to take the Pensacola pulse.

Thirty-three miles eastward along the ICW are the twin communities of Fort Walton Beach and Destin, which are separated by East Pass. Some cruisers prefer to go out at Pensacola and sail down to East Pass at Destin, though it is a somewhat longer distance. It can be a difficult pass in hard southerlies and the current can run hard.

Sailboat skippers foreign to the area who desire to use East Pass should first check the fixed bridge clearance. I have seen different clearance figures given, but in mid-summer 1980 Destin marinas agreed it was 48 feet.

Fort Walton Beach

Intracoastal waterways are essential to recreational boats in Florida; otherwise, in a peninsula-shaped state, all the cruising would be done in open waters, which would eliminate a sizable percentage of those who like their boating in reasonably protected waters. One of the drawbacks, however, is that there is an inclination to "ride the range" of the channel without turning off to investigate potential places of interest to port or starboard.

Those who tire of miles of mangroves, cabbage palms and scrub oak in the central to lower part of Florida cruising waters would find a welcome change of pace and scenery by cruising northwest to north of the ICW at Fort Walton Beach and the west end of big Choctawhatchee Bay.

It's bayou country, where tall pines ring the shore, along with dozens of "summer places" complete with boathouses. It is reminiscent of "north country" cruising, so unlike most of Florida seen by water that the temptation is to think that, somehow, somewhere, the state line was crossed without anyone noticing it.

Unfortunately, some of the bayous are blocked by fixed bridges, with a vertical clearance of only 19 feet. Examination of area charts, however, will show bayous that do not have bridges. Most of them have deep water—plenty for sailboats—with numerous good anchorages. Cruising boats seem to be welcome, or so we judged by one incident. In Rocky Bayou, two pleasant teenagers swam out 100 yards or so to say hello and accepted our invitation to come aboard for a visit.

One side cruise, not complicated by bridges, is up Boggy Bayou, seven miles northeast of Choctawhatchee Bay. There are two communities along the way, Valparaiso on the west bank, at the intersection with Toms Bayou, and Niceville, at the head of the bayou.

We recall cruising *Final Edition* to Niceville one Sunday morning in July. The sky was cloudless, the water calm enough to catch some of the shoreline reflections. The tall pines seemed to have grown as if in parade ground military formation, uniformly spaced, erect. Here and there ranks had been broken for the building of a summer home.

As we approached Niceville—the name seemed so appropriate—we could hear the church bells ringing. People were entering the First Baptist church, a large, white, wooden building. Farther along we

Anyone home at No. 17? Located on the lawn of a Fort Walton Beach residence, No. 17 is a flashing light navigation aid just off the Gulf Intracoastal Waterway. It is one of the few waterway aids that has to have the grass around it cut periodically. Marston photo

could see another building with a sign that read Deliverance Temple.

Berthed alongside a dock farther up was a brand new shrimp boat, still being fitted out, with a hull painted so bright red it reflected a circular patch of fire on the stilled waters. The name on the transom was *Crimson Lady*; that, she was. Some days are made for pictures.

The Intracoastal between Pensacola and Fort Walton Beach is used by most transient boats. It may not be the most exciting cruising but it is most unusual. Much of it passes through miles of the U.S. Eglin Air Force Base, the largest in the world. On the north side of Choctawhatchee Bay are many more miles of the Eglin influence. There are anchoring restrictions, and good reasons for them in the military zones. But scan the skies while running the Eglin section of the ICW;

you may see unusual aircraft aloft, some doing unusual things.

A few years ago we were at anchor aboard *Final Edition* in a permitted Eglin area. While out on deck, enjoying the cool evening breeze, watching the stars, Peggy's attention was attracted to a plane in the night sky. She kept her binoculars on it for a rather long time but finally said, "That airplane has been flying backwards part of the time. I've been watching its running lights. I am sure it stops and reverses direction without turning." I looked but could not see what she was seeing. The matter was finally dismissed with a general comment, something like, "Well, I suppose anything is possible at Eglin." But, really now, flying backwards?

A couple of years later, cruising up the Intracoastal Waterway near Swansboro, N.C., we were startled to see military planes making vertical takeoffs. "If they do that, maybe they can fly backwards; maybe that plane at Eglin *was* flying backwards," said Peggy. Today, we all know there are military planes capable of braking to a halt in the air, flying backwards and maneuvering sideways.

Destin

Any list of top fishing locations in the United States that does not include Destin is incomplete. In the summer months it may be the premier place of all. Only in recent years has Destin—and Panama City should probably be co-listed, since much of the same waters are fished in the Gulf of Mexico—received its just due. In the past, the more year-round, concentrated charterboat fleets at Palm Beach, Stuart, Islamorada and other Florida Keys fishing points previously diluted statewide attention.

Not only does Destin have outstanding offshore fishing for sailfish, blue and white marlin, but close to the beaches there's good seasonal action for king mackerel and Spanish mackerel. And, as is the case off Panama City Beach, there is a spring run of cobia, also known as ling, that draws hordes of fishermen. For those who prefer bottom fishing, there are grouper, red snapper and amberjack, among others.

The charter fleet at Destin numbers around 120. Private craft that come in for the summer fishing are numerous. It is not impossible for a transient to get a berth, but it is best to call ahead. Another suggestion is to try the collection of marinas at Fort Walton Beach. Many have space allocated for cruising craft.

Another good choice is Destin's Old Pass Lagoon, protected, right on the edge of the Gulf. It is virtually a landlocked harbor; anchoring stern-to the lagoon beach is popular.

We recall the days when the Destin fishing fleet was primarily commercial. There were many party or "head" boats, the term coming from passengers being charged so much a head. The sportsfishing boats came along later. When the great old husband and wife team of Smokey and Edna Jones came into Destin with outriggers, they were laughed at by some. Old timers wouldn't believe fish could be caught on those "fold-out sticks." Today, a forest of outriggers rings the charterboat docks.

Good fishing and beautiful beaches put Destin on the map, more so than some of the long term residents like. From a community of around 800 in the 1950s, the number of regular residents rose to 6,000 in the late '70s. In the summer, there's an influx of 14,000 more people.

The name comes from Leonard Destin, a New England seafaring man who arrived in the 1830s and stayed to found a village. Since then, seven generations of Destins have lived on the narrow peninsula between the Gulf of Mexico and Choctawhatchee Bay.

Choctawhatchee Bay

This bay, 25 miles long, provides many bayous to poke in and out of and plenty of deep water for sailing. Fort Walton Beach is at the west end; Eglin AFB occupies most of the north shore. The south shore is liberally sprinkled with bayous; one of the most popular is Joe's Bayou, a snug anchorage in most winds, and further popular because of its close proximity to shopping at Destin.

Florida's Grand Canyon

"This is the tug *Jo-Jo* entering the Grand Canyon," announced its captain in a matter-of-fact voice. What would the Grand Canyon be doing in Florida? Peggy and I were momentarily puzzled but when *Jo-Jo*'s skipper came back again on the marine radio to give his exact position in relation to a mileage point and a bridge on the Gulf Intracoastal, we understood.

Jo-Jo was just starting into a land cut nearly 20 miles long. The tug had left the West Bay section traveling westbound and would emerge at Choctawhatchee Bay. The 20-mile distance in between was called the Grand Canyon.

The "canyon" reference is not a complete misnomer. A long section of the cut runs through high, sandy cliffs. Dredging for the Gulf Intracoastal laid bare the cliffs' soil strata below a thin forested carpeting. Half-exposed roots of tilted pines grasp the shifting soil in a tenacious struggle to keep the trees from tumbling down into the waterway. The winter winds and squalls of summer erode the earth. Periodic torrential rains carve deep scars on the white sandy faces of the cliffs which, in some places, rise 60 to 70 feet above the water.

Behind the cliffs lie swamps, one of them referred to on the chart as "impenetrable." Drainage pipes protruding from the canyon walls offer the only other clue to the presence of swamps.

The U.S. Corps of Engineers is charged with housekeeping the Gulf Intracoastal, an endless task because of landslides, trees, broken limbs and other debris that fall into the waterway. Cruising boats frequently need to be steered around floating logs and should maintain a watch for debris that may lie just under the surface.

In 1975, extraordinarily heavy rains caused a major landslide that blocked the Intracoastal in the Grand Canyon. The waterway was closed for weeks while dredges, working from both ends of the slide, struggled to create an opening.

The landslide had been cleared away only a short time when Hurricane Eloise appeared, giving the beach communities between Panama City and Fort Walton Beach a September thrashing that left 17,000 homeless and ran property damage to over $100 million.

The 200 miles of waterway between Pensacola and Carrabelle is a pleasurable cruise, made more so by the addition of prior knowledge. The most protected area is between Apalachicola and Choctawhatchee Bay. Panama City is the pivot point, lying between West Bay and East Bay.

There are six major canals or creeks in the waterway between Apalachicola and Choctawhatchee Bay. Here, one is certain to meet tug and barge combinations, but most of the tugs have wheelhouses high above the water and usually the captain can see you long before you are aware of his presence.

Radio communication is important on the Gulf Intracoastal, not only in the hidden areas such as the Grand Canyon, but also when passing situations occur.

Today, most recreational craft have VHF-FM radios, which can bridge the communications gap that once existed between pleasure

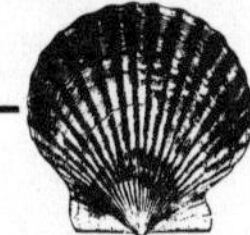

boats and commercial vessels. This comparatively new relationship is necessary to good operations, in the Gulf Intracoastal in particular. Channel 16 should be kept on at all times. The tugs monitor it as well as the Coast Guard. Switching channels include 6, 9, 12, 13 and 68. Channel 6 is not often used and is generally clear for boat-to-boat traffic. As an example of how well this works, back when our friend *Jo-Jo* entered the canyon, we called to establish our relationship with her position. That exchange produced a call to the tug and to *Final Edition* from a Coast Guard buoy tender a few miles behind which would have gradually overtaken us.

Later, we picked up a position report from a tug headed towards us, learned that she was pushing a long, heavy barge that would need any bend in the waterway all to herself. By radio and chart, I was able to find a spot where I could pull *Final Edition* off to the side, well back from the turn in the channel.

Watch for blind corners. Assume that a boat may be approaching unseen. In any meeting with a tug that is turning, or preparing to turn, remember that, unlike the automobile that tracks tight, the tug's stern sweeps wide before it can straighten up for the next course. It may be that passing starboard-to-starboard is advisable. Ask the tug captain on which side of his vessel and tow he'd prefer you to be.

When overtaking a tug traveling slower than you, call for permission to pass. The captain may know something you don't. From his elevated wheelhouse he can see far ahead; his radio information may be better than yours.

Never try to pass on a turn; wait for a long straightaway. Anyone who has passed a two- or three-section barge at eight knots while the tug is pushing its load at six will confirm that it takes more than two or three minutes. It's up to you to find the room to pass. A loaded tug is going to be in the deepest part of the waterway, where it has to be.

Panama City

This important port for pleasure and commercial craft is about 15 miles short of being halfway between Pensacola and Carrabelle. It is a "must" stop for transients needing supplies, to pick up mail, change crews, or just as a logical stop between two distant points.

While some transients find it difficult to get berths there, it may be related to the marinas being spread out and inconveniently located for those who just wish to turn off the Intracoastal and make a quick connection. Our stops have always been at St. Andrews Marina. Circumstances once dictated that we remain there for a month, a stay that permitted us to get to know some of the local people, including the Davis brothers who operate the marina and head a fleet of party fishing boats.

Panama City is a major fishing center, on the order of Destin. The charterboats are located on the city waterfront and out on Panama City Beach. The Anderson family, owner of a large fleet of party boats, have been berthed at the beach for many years. The return of the Anderson and Davis boats every afternoon in the summer always produces a throng of the curious.

There are acceptable-to-good anchorages between the mainland and the barrier beaches. South of the entrance is Shell Island, which we found to be a good anchorage. Others in the area near the St. Andrews Bay Yacht Club include Watson, Massalina and Smack bayous. It was at St. Andrews that the earliest British settlement was made in 1765, though the Spanish had already been there, between 1516 and 1540.

It's 50 miles along the Gulf Intracoastal to Apalachicola. About 23 miles west of that city, the five-mile-long Gulf County Canal leads from the waterway to Port St. Joe, the scene of one of the most tragic stories in Florida's history.

DEATH OF ST. JOSEPH CITY

Chapter 5

In the decade beginning in 1840, the bright, young and promising Gulf coast city of St. Joseph literally died. Hundreds of citizens—some estimates run as high as 3,000—perished. A raging epidemic of yellow fever, two hurricanes and a fire destroyed the city that hoped to rival Apalachicola as a port for cotton and become a fashionable resort for the wealthy. Evangelists proclaimed God killed St. Joseph because it was a wicked city.

Today, countless boats cruise right past Port St. Joe, the new city that rose from the ashes of the dead. Few are aware of the horror that transpired over 100 years ago.

From a cruising standpoint, the city itself has nothing to offer. There's a too-small, though amiably operated, boat basin, a huge pulp mill (indeed, the St. Joe Paper Co. is the heartbeat of the town.) and a chemical plant along the waterfront, hardly a combination that would entice anyone looking for a good cruising stop.

Yet, three miles westward across the bay is a little-known jewel in Florida's cruising crown, a peninsula that extends for miles, the long arm of narrow land jutting up from the elbow of Cape San Blas. On the chart it is shown as St. Joseph Spit.

Commercial fishing at Port St. Joe has been a way of life for decades, headquartered on the Gulf County Canal north of St. Joseph Bay. Local fishermen have a reputation for helping transient boaters find an emergency overnight berth.
Florida Division of Tourism photo

The Gulf of Mexico lies on its west side, its waves washing ashore on 20 unbroken miles of beautiful beach. On the east is 12-mile-long St. Joseph Bay, one of the best natural harbors in the state. Near mid-peninsula is small, but well protected, Eagle Harbor. Directly ashore is a 2,500-acre state park with miles of white, uncluttered beaches, beautiful clear water, good fishing, scalloping and clamming. Despite all this, the attractive harbor, and wooded peninsula dotted with high, sandy dunes, are not well known to cruisers.

Some advantages are provided for those who come by boat. There are ramps and docks for small craft and a concession center. The area serves as a gathering point for exchange of information.

The road approaches to the park lead from Port St. Joe and Apalachicola. The highway access makes it convenient for friends or family members to join a cruising group at Eagle Harbor.

It took us a while to "discover" St. Joseph peninsula, and it is a continuing regret that we did not allow enough time to stay longer.

Port St. Joe has outgrown its tragic background, though, technically, old St. Joseph and new Port St. Joe were never one and the same. Still, the present city geographically straddles its fated predecessor.

For a small town, it has been much in the news over the years, a community with more than its share of racial unrest. In the 1960s, it was the controversial case of Freddie Pitts and Wilbert Lee.

Pitts and Lee, both black, were convicted by an all-white jury in 1963 for the murders of two service station attendants in Port St. Joe. They spent 12 years in jail—10 of them on death row—but in 1975, then-Governor Reubin Askew and the State Cabinet freed the pair after another prisoner confessed to the slayings.

The liberal newspapers had been charging all along that Pitts and Lee were framed by small town prejudices, that there had been a miscarriage of justice. The release from jail of the two blacks made national headlines and created widespread editorial comment; so did their petition for damages in the amount of $100,000 each for their long incarceration.

By night, from a boat quietly anchored in Eagle Harbor across the bay, the brilliantly lighted pulp mill can be seen steaming and smoking away. Its loom is seen for miles far at sea. The peacefulness of the scene is in sharp contrast with the struggles of Port St. Joe.

Old St. Joseph

Developers in the early 1840s had had great dreams for St. Joseph. Young, ambitious, she was well-positioned on the edge of the sparkling Gulf waters. Her creators envisioned her as a natural beauty, in position to become a great resort on the railway between Charleston and New Orleans.

She had already gained a measure of fame, thanks to the inspired promoters who had managed to make her the site for the state constitutional convention of 1838, despite the obviously better location of Tallahassee. (Local enterprise had seen to it that St. Joseph had a hall for the convention.)

St. Joseph was actually created by a group of unhappy citizens of Apalachicola who felt they had been designated virtual squatters after a land ruling by the U.S. Supreme Court had gone against them. They decided to go about 20 miles northwest, along the coast, and start a new town on St. Joseph Bay.

St. Joseph did prosper for a time, but it never became another Apalachicola. There were splendid homes with walled gardens, new hotels of brick construction and a quay that extended out into the bay. There were warehouses, business buildings, several churches, two horse race tracks and, predictably, a number of taverns and saloons, not unlike commercial ports around the world.

But in the summer of 1841, everything was to change. A sailing vessel from South America rounded St. Joseph Point one sultry July day, and dropped anchor. Soon, word was sent the captain was dead of yellow fever. The disease came ashore and struck the town with devastating force.

G. M. West in his pamphlet, "Old St. Joe," presents a particularly elaborate account using original information from the Pensacola *Gazette* of August 7, 1841:

"Daily showers had filled the various marshes surrounding the city; the moist, hot air was sweltering and depressing. Swarms of mosquitos rose from their many breeding places in marshes and swamps, as well as from the numerous ditches that interlaced the city; so many messengers of death. To be stricken was to die.

"Secretly, silently, this fateful guest stalked through the busy streets, stole into stores and offices, *tete-a-teted* with the beauty and

the chivalry of the city at charming entertainments and frolicked with old and young in this memorable year of 1841.

"One morning the news fled through the city that there had been a death from yellow fever. Bankers ceased counting money and discounting bills, lawyers laid aside their briefs and turned their thoughts to this unconquered enemy of mankind. Doctors pored over their books and papers reaching for their unobtainable knowledge wherewith to combat successfully the mortal disease.

"The newspaper stopped its press that it might insert the news. Merchants quit offering their wares, wondering what the outcome might be while mothers clasped closer their offspring thinking thereby to shield them from impending danger.

"Other days passed and more deaths were announced. Processions to the burying grounds beyond the cypress swamp at the rear of the city became frequent. The powers of the Negro grave diggers were taxed to the utmost to open sufficient graves for the oft-recurring processions. The limited stock of coffins was exhausted.

"The high carnival of death had opened most auspiciously. It had already eclipsed and ended all festivities. Cheeks that were but the day before flushed with youth and beauty now blanched with fear. Uncontrollable fear seized upon all. Business ceased. Ships slipped their anchors and stole away into the night. The air was stagnant and filled with pestilential vapors.

"Many sought safety through flight, only to be stricken and die by the wayside. Soon the horrid pestilence held undisputed sway throughout the city. Deaths were no longer counted. All day long was heard the rumble of the death wagons upon the streets. Trenches took the places of graves, and rude boxes of coffins.

"Half-crazed, men would rush to the surrounding woods for safety with heads bursting with inexpressible pain, and eyes forcing themselves from their sockets. Under some lofty pine, they would check their mad flight, hesitate, stagger, then the dark blood, the black vomit of death, would come rushing through their parched lips. They would fall forward into this pool of deadened blood—and die. Great God, what a death!

"The heretofore prosperous city was doomed. The death angel held undisputed sway. As he passed from door to door he found no blood-stained lintel as in the days of yore. Few were spared. Families were broken up by flight—only to be soon reunited in death. How quickly love, hatred, the passion for wealth, or learning, were placed in one common receptacle!

"How insignificant was man. Reason, humanity, charity, all had fled. Like the dumb brute of the woods or field, man died uncared for and alone. In a very brief space of time the city was depopulated ... the famed city of St. Joseph was dead."

The abject misery of those still alive after the yellow fever siege was compounded by a September hurricane that came roaring in off the Gulf. Damage would have been greater but many of the sailing vessels had already fled St. Joseph. Some time after that there was a fire to add to the torment of those still trying to hang on.

The last blow was another hurricane, on September 8, 1844. Surging over St. Joseph Spit, it came crashing into the battered city. There really was not much left for the storm to destroy. The young city that grew old so fast had already been thinned of abandoned homes.

Residents of nearby Apalachicola bought many of the houses, and shipped them in pieces by schooner back to the very city many of the former owners had left.

About the same time the Great Revival Age started and St. Joseph was proclaimed a wicked place. Lorna Carroll, a writer for the St. Petersburg *Times*, wrote: "In the end the Four Horsemen of the Apocalypse galloped down her gaudy streets, lashing to the left and right with whips of hurricane, fire, plague and flood, burying her under sand. Folks said she was dead and gone for good, that all her cheap beauty would rot beneath the sand like her plague-ridden inhabitants, shoveled into trenches up in the cemetery."

St. Joseph lay undeveloped until 1906, when T. H. Stone started to promote the area under the name of Port St. Joe. The reborn community developed first as a fishing village, and later, because of the surrounding forest, as a sawmill site.

In 1936, the St. Joe Paper Company was formed and the town turned the corner toward progress.

The St. Joe museum is a monument to the birth struggle for Florida's statehood. A well-kept cemetery is the surviving symbol of the young city that died before its time and rose again.

Medicine Man of St. Vincent Island

St. Vincent Island, an island with a colorful history, is a national wildlife refuge, four miles wide at its eastern end, nine miles long overall. No permission is needed to go ashore, to walk the beaches, to surf fish, watch birdlife or take pictures. A permit is required, however, to visit the interior of the 12,358-acre island, obtained by

writing Refuge Manager, P.O. Box 447, Apalachicola Fla., 32320.

There is no Florida barrier island quite like it. Unlike some of the long sandy strands that are barren of vegetation, St. Vincent is a grand mixture of tidal marshes, fresh water pools (fishing permitted March 1 through October 31), acres of magnolia trees, pines, cabbage palms and at least three types of oak trees—live, turkey and scrub. There are ridges of scrub oak, pine flatwoods and hammocks well populated with palm and magnolia. (Any summertime venture into the interior is an encounter with an assortment of unrelenting insects. Go prepared.)

Peggy and I toured St. Vincent in 1973 with Don Temple, a dedicated U.S. Fish and Wildlife worker. It was a jeep tour during which we saw deer, several types of wading birds, wild hogs and the largest wild turkey I had ever seen. We looked for, but did not see, a sambar, a large deer native to Asia, although a few were known to be on the island.

At one time, the island was owned by Dr. Ray V. Pierce, the patent medicine king. Old-timers will remember Dr. Pierce's Pleasant Purgative Pellets and Dr. Pierce's Golden Medical Discovery.

In his day, Dr. Pierce imported several exotic species of animals to St. Vincent, including zebra, eland, black buck and the sambar.

Dr. Pierce died on the island in 1914 and in 1948 it was sold to Alfred and Henry Loomis of New York City, known to many as prominent yachtsmen. Later, as the Loomis brothers observed developers and special interest groups taking over land and beaches, they arranged to sell the island to the U.S. Bureau of Sport Fisheries and Wildlife, and thus, it became a national wildlife refuge.

Although only a few of the black buck and sambars remain, the refuge is home for a wide variety of animals, birds, and even alligators in the fresh water areas. Sea turtles come ashore to lay their eggs. As Peggy and I rode along the beach with Temple, we saw three places where turtles had laid eggs, each marked by a stake bearing the date of the egg laying. A heavy protective wire screen lay over the nests, to keep wild hogs from the eggs.

Before Dr. Pierce, the island had been purchased at auction for $3,000 by Charles Hatch, one-time mayor of Cincinnati. From Hatch it was bought by an old Confederate general, and then in 1907, that enterprising Yankee Dr. Pierce bought it.

Sale terms have varied in values over the years. In the early 1800s, 22 Seminole Indian chiefs traded the island and much other Panhandle land to white traders in exchange for settling their tribal debts to them. In the latest transaction, the Loomis brothers sold it to the federal government for $2.2 million. It was a bargain price.

Nearly 10 years later, Florida taxpayers paid four times that much for one-sixth as much land: $8.8 million for just 2,100 acres on nearby St. George Island.

From St. Joseph peninsula, it is a good-weather-only cruise down around Cape San Blas to St. Vincent. Pick a clear, windless day with the sun overhead by the time Cape San Blas shoals are reached. Chart study will show a swash channel that may be used. The objective is West Pass, which lies between St. Vincent and the northwest tip of St. George Island. West Pass leads into Apalachicola Bay, with Apalachicola itself only nine miles away. The alternative is to use the Gulf County Canal and return to the Gulf Intracoastal.

APALACHICOLA COPS AND OYSTERS

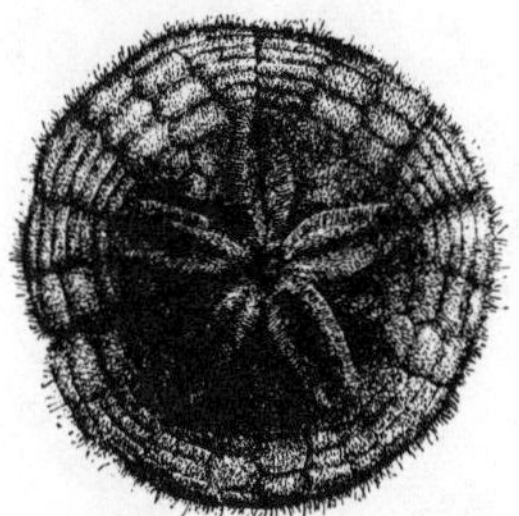

Chapter 6

Between Apalachicola and Carrabelle, flanked by 24-mile-long St. George Island, lies one of Florida's finest cruising areas. Apalachicola Bay and St. George Sound provide 40 miles of water between the mainland and the elongated island that is one of the most imposing of the many barrier islands in the state.

Not only does the composition of St. George Island, the sound that bears its name and the 280 square miles of Apalachicola Bay provide a recreational bonanza, the local economy is geared to it.

Oystering is the economic backbone of the entire area. Local cars carry bumper stickers that read, "Oysters Make Better Lovers." A poor oyster yield does to Apalachicola, Carrabelle and East Point what a prolonged drought does to farming communities of the Midwest.

Fresh water, notably from the Apalachicola River but augmented by others that flow into East Bay, feeds the ecological system with the balance it needs to supply 85 percent of the state's oyster production.

While in other parts of the nation a certain amount of acclaim goes to the fastest herring packer or the swiftest chicken plucker, around Apalachicola it's the national oyster shucking champion. Heidi Harrelson is a local celebrity because she won the national title in 1979, beating the best Chesapeake Bay could put up against her.

St. George Sound and Apalachicola Bay, varying in width from three to six miles, are separated from the Gulf of Mexico not only by St. George Island but also by Dog Island at the east end and St. Vincent on the west.

The Gulf Intracoastal Waterway connecting Apalachicola and Carrabelle goes through the sound and bay. The markers are far apart in some areas, making a compass course a good backup if bad weather should close in. Though the islands protect those on the waterway from heavy seas, there are places where, with a long fetch, the wind can make the 30 miles between the two cities a wet, choppy ride.

A bridge, nine miles east of Apalachicola with a fixed vertical clearance of 50 feet, connects the mainland, at the commercial fishing community of East Point, with St. George Island. It is also the dividing line between the sound and the bay.

The bay, the sound and either side of St. George Island present excellent cruising and fishing opportunities, as well as shelling, crabbing, oystering, swimming, beach walking and even driftwood-gathering that, collectively, probably cannot be surpassed in any other place in Florida.

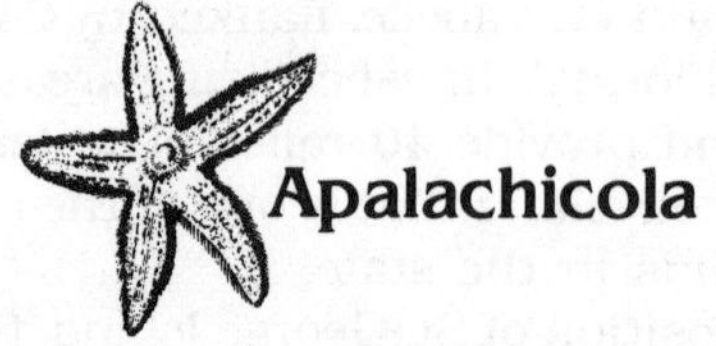

Apalachicola

It's an old waterfront city, chartered in 1831, that has yo-yo'd through history. It's been wild and been subdued, burned out and blown out, yet will probably be around as long as there are oysters left in the bay, grouper and snapper in the Gulf and timber still to be cut.

There was a time, not so many years ago, when cruising people couldn't find a place to stay overnight. The city marina was crowded with local commercial craft. Now, the municipal marina has been revamped, and fundamental facilities such as power and water are provided visiting yachts.

In addition, the Rainbow Marina and Motel complex built in the mid-70s on the Apalachicola River waterfront, is where a large percentage of cruising boat skippers make it a point to stay. Here, one can rest up, walk around historic old Apalachicola, wait out a brief spell of bad weather, eat seafood and, if lucky enough to be there in the right season, catch up on oyster eating.

The Dr. John Gorrie Museum, no more than a 10-minute walk from the Rainbow or the city marina at Battery Park, commemorates his invention of a "cooling machine," an 1839 discovery that opened the way for today's modern refrigeration and air conditioning principles. Next time you put ice cubes in a drink, remember Dr. Gorrie.

In the early 1830s, Apalachicola was the third largest port in the United States. Forty three-story brick warehouses, all in a row, were built along the Apalachicola River.

New England Yankees, with their penchant for being where the action is, came early. In 1893, Cosam Emir Bartlett operated a weekly newspaper called the Apalachicola *Gazette*, which later became the first newspaper in Florida published on a daily basis.

Apalachicola's reign as a great cotton, shipping and trading port ended with the coming of railroads, but not before waterfront lots sold for $10,000 in 1800s dollars and the lively river delta town became the scene of lavish antebellum society and wealth.

By 1860, Apalachicola was the second largest port on the west coast of Florida, though not up to the peak reached in the 1830s, when as many as 140 ships stood by in the bay waiting their turn to load or unload their cargo.

When the cotton trade disappeared, some said Apalachicola's

A series of fires in the early days of Apalachicola destroyed churches, the opera house and businesses. Some stately old homes also burned, but there were survivors. One is the century-old "Steamboat House," so named because it reminded some residents of the superstructure of an elaborate river boat.
Marston photo

reason for living was gone. It, too, suffered a siege of yellow fever, fires and hurricanes. Lumbering eventually replaced cotton as the big industry, and faded.

In May of 1900, another fire roared through Apalachicola, burning or gutting the opera house, armory, churches, stately homes and buildings along the river. Some of those scars can be seen today.

While Apalachicola's residential past has not yet undergone any major restoration effort, historical awareness has been on the rise. Homes over 100 years old that survived the fires are now marked with a gold star. Those over 90 years old rate a blue star.

One of the major edifices that survived the fire of 1900 was Trinity Episcopal Church, possibly the oldest pre-fab building in the country. In 1838 it was shipped in sections by boat from New England and is still in use. It is open to visitors, its condition is maintained and its hand-hewn interiors are fascinating. The church is a 10-minute walk from the waterfront.

James Daily, twice mayor of Apalachicola, born in the city and devoted to it, has become one of the foremost active citizens in promoting historical recognition.

Paradoxical as it may seem, some measure of Apalachicola's future

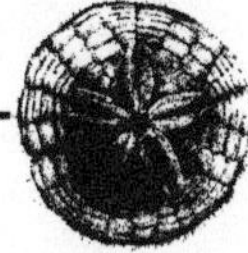

may lie in its past. History may be difficult to market but it has proven successful for several waterfront cities, notably Boston and Baltimore. There can be a profitable—as well as educational—side to restoration.

Some view Apalachicola as poor but peaceful, its slow pace a redeeming feature. "If Apalach grows too big, the oysters and shrimp may leave us and we will be left with nothing but history, which cannot be eaten," one resident told us.

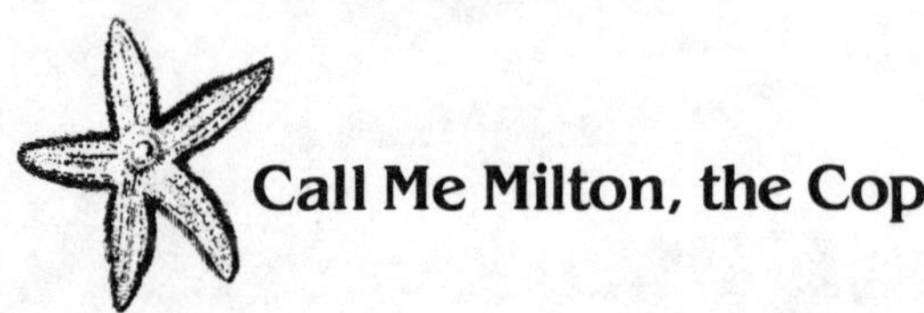

Call Me Milton, the Cop

Not every small town has a cop who will take your wife grocery shopping in the police cruiser. For that matter, not many towns will open the post office after hours to let a stranger collect mail, either.

Peggy and I brought *Final Edition* into Apalachicola for the first time in May of 1973. We eased the 38-footer into the small city marina crowded with small local commercial boats and a handful of pleasure craft. We tied up in the one vacant space temporarily; then, after hearing the owner of the space wouldn't be back for several days, we tied up more securely.

An hour or so later, Peggy and I were uptown with our two-wheeled, collapsible cart, to do some grocery shopping and to pick up waiting mail. Right away we discovered the post office was closed.

As we stood on a corner, revising our plans, a postal jeep stopped at a pickup box near us. We remarked to the driver we couldn't get mail at the post office. He smiled and said, "Come around the back way in about 10 minutes. I'll get your mail."

A few minutes later, an Apalachicola police cruiser drove up and the driver called out, "Are you the folks that own *Final Edition* down in the yacht basin?" I read a sense of emergency into the tone of his voice. The dire possibilities immediately sprinted through my mind... it's sinking... it broke loose, rammed another boat... no, not a fire, we'd have heard the volunteer fire department.

"I'm sorry, but you'll have to move your boat. The man who rents the space just came back in his houseboat and he wants in," said the officer. Peggy said she'd like to get some grocery shopping done first, if possible.

"Well, pile in here," said the cop. "Put that cart in back. I'll take you to the grocery store, then I'll go down to see if the man will wait a few minutes. He's an executive in one of the big lumber companies here."

We met the officer on the way back. He pulled over and said, "I told him you all were just staying overnight, so he agreed to stay where he is over on the other side of the basin. But if you have an extra length of electric cord, he could use it."

Of course we had extra cord aboard, as do most who cruise into strange places where the extent of marina facilities is uncertain. We apologized to the owner of the space for inconveniencing him. He graciously replied, "It was my fault. I should have put up a sign saying the space is private."

It occurs to us from time to time that people down by the water seem to be able to work out their small problems with a minimum of conflict. Usurping someone's parking space, even unintentionally, in some metropolitan cities could lead to jack-handle warfare.

That evening, the police cruiser stopped alongside *Final Edition.* Out stepped the officer who had taken us shopping earlier in the day, to collect the dock space rent (all of $3, electricity included). As he started to leave, I realized I didn't know his name. "Just call me Milton, the Cop," he said with a smile.

In subsequent stops at Apalachicola, we made a point of looking Milton up. Each time it seemed he had been promoted a rank or two. Then, in the fall of 1979, we learned Milton, the Cop, had become Milton Houseman, chief of the Apalachicola Police Department.

Other pleasant associations are connected with cruising into Apalachicola. There was the time when J. V. "Bubba" Gander, the Gulf fuel dealer, made room for *Final Edition* at his dock, even though it was spring and a busy time for him.

Gander was program chairman for the Rotary Club. One day he reported that the scheduled speaker was called out of town on some emergency. Would I pinch-hit? I was to discover the old time art of dickering was not out of fashion in Apalachicola. I showed up as the Rotary Club speaker and Bubba Gander didn't charge me for dockage.

Some people who visit Apalachicola go only once a year—usually, the first Saturday in November when all roads lead to the Apalachicola Seafood Festival. Thousands swarm into a community that is normally geared to only 3,000 people.

Festivities include a street parade ending at Battery Park on the waterfront; seafood, prepared many ways, sold at church-operated booths; an oyster shucking contest; a castnet throwing competition; street concerts; gospel singing; a blue crab race; oyster eating championships; a sidewalk art show; politicians orating; the blessing of the shrimp fleet and a grand ball for the finale.

Anyone still hungry can always visit one of the small, five- or six-seat oyster bars on the main highway leading west of town. Oysters are opened before your eyes as fast as you can eat them. Many local oyster experts chase the oysters down with a beer. There's a reason for that. The brew comes in handy as a diluter after the oysters have been sloshed around in a red-hot concoction called Tiger Sauce.

St. George Island

If a cruising addict were to ask for one island to keep a family occupied with interesting things from spring through fall, St. George would be a logical choice. Nearly all the "Florida" things you are supposed to do with and from a cruising boat can be done around St. George.

The state park on the east end of the island has seven miles of frontage on the Gulf and nearly 12 miles on St. George Sound. It is an immense piece of recreational property—1500 acres—yet miles of St. George's beach and shoreline are left for those who wish to be independent of other visitors.

St. George is really two islands. A dredged cut through the land, locally called the Bob Sikes cut and named for a former congressman from the Panhandle, created the islands. It is the main entrance to Apalachicola from the Gulf. The city is so positioned it can claim that 100 miles of shoreline lie within a 10-mile radius of it.

At the western end, easily reached from Apalachicola, is Cape St. George where a lighthouse rises 72 feet above the water. This area is more remote than the larger, eastern section and can be reached only by boat. The beach is said to be one of the better shelling areas along the northwest Florida coast.

East of Sikes cut is a beach community of summer homes and a few year-round residences. At the island end of the bridge and causeway is a small marina, and a community settlement center where general information may be obtained.

Rugged as the island is, history has proved that it cannot completely withstand a major hurricane. In 1972 Hurricane Agnes demolished the road, now rebuilt, leading to the east end. Nevertheless, the 24-mile island is an effective barrier, and prevents the mainland from taking the full brunt of a storm.

Such barrier islands are, in effect, large sandbars that are unstable through constant erosion and shifting. Their shapes change from the force of storms, pounding surf, ocean currents and the slowly rising sea level. Their vulnerability is increasingly coming to the attention of concerned federal authorities who feel that extensive development of such islands is so hazardous that controls may have to be placed on their expansion. Government purchase of more of these islands is a possibility, but in the case of St. George, the presence of the large state park already reduces the development potential.

Dog Island

East of St. George Island is Dog Island, smaller and only six miles from Carrabelle. The island has a ferry service and an airstrip for small planes.

The Dog Island Company, which controls development of the island, directs its operation towards weekend and vacation retreats thus preventing overcrowding, even in the peak summer months. There are a few accommodations, including rooms for rent, an island restaurant or two and limited supplies. The beaches are good. So is the fishing, seasonally. If you go, follow the marked ferry boat channel in. Staying time may be limited at the dock but one is welcome all the same. At the west end of Dog Island there is a little hook inside which boats frequently anchor. The holding ground is good. We have spent some pleasant days and nights there, sometimes surrounded by clusters of shrimp boats. Shrimping is done at night; the crews sleep by day.

Home-owners on the island, certainly at the west end, have always been friendly and last we heard were not discouraging boat people from coming ashore by dinghy as long as their privacy was respected.

We were curious to find how the island got its name. Jeff Lewis, a Tallahassee banker who did much to establish the Dog Island community, told us that a chart dated 1690 showed a group of islands in the general area called Isle aux Chiens (Island of Dogs). Very likely wild dogs did roam the area at one time.

The island has two coves, one named Ballast and the other Shipping. At one time, Ballast was a dumping ground in the 1800s for ballast rock brought in on sailing ships from all over the world. Shipping Cove was the gathering place for vessels taking on lumber and naval stores brought out from Carrabelle. During World War II, Dog Island was an amphibious landing training area.

Carrabelle

Carrabelle is an active commercial fishing and oystering port. The harbor is well protected and the entrance easy to locate by its relationship to the Crooked River light that is 2.3 miles west of Carrabelle.

The city from time to time received a smattering of national publicity because its police station was a telephone booth. Call the listed police number and you would get a pay station. A police officer, stationed in a parked cruiser, answered the phone. In a community of about 1,500 people, where everyone knows each other, it was possible to cut down on the overhead using the dial-a-cop system.

Carrabelle, however, is best known to countless cruisers as a jumping-off point for the Big Bend passage. Late starters caught in the nor'westers in early December or the latter part of November have frequently been weathered in at Carrabelle for days at a time. Limited space, however, has created a problem for transients. One marina was forced out of business when erosion blocked its entrance and damaged its bulkheads. Another large marina has been operating for years, but dock space is limited, and boats are required to raft up in bad weather. As a result, some skippers who make the Big Bend run, especially those taking the offshore route, have switched to Apalachicola as a departure point.

One possible solution to the dock space problem is to go under the high level bridge over the Carrabelle River and anchor up river. From here, six-foot depths take you to the confluence of the New and Crooked rivers. We took *Final Edition* up for a look-around. There are places to anchor there, but it appeared to us there could be a problem with currents near the river bends.

Small town waterfronts are seldom without a local philosopher. Carrabelle's most noted is Noah Oswald Cook, several-time mayor of Carrabelle. Al Burt, of the Miami *Herald*, interviewed Cook one day and found Noah in a reflective mood.

"You don't know a person any more; you just know of them," he said. "Back in my day, our vocabulary was small. Now it's growed to a tremendous vocabulary. But it's kinda like teaching a parakeet to talk. He talks and that's as far as he can go. No action. Makes it bad.

"It's pitiful to me how some people has got education and all that book learnin' and still don't know anything. The only people that

Carrabelle is an important port for cruising skippers planning to cross the long, open Big Bend area and continue on to South Florida. Bad weather is waited out here. Carrabelle's principal industries are seafood processing and commercial fishing. It is also the base for several party fishing boats.
Florida Division of Tourism photo

thrived during the Depression was people who couldn't write their own name. But they knowed how to make money, not paper business. Now, everything's done on paper."

Noah Oswald Cook longs for more practical times, yet sees the world being taken over by "fast-talking parakeets." And he'll tell you that it was Thomas Edison who observed that any person who spoke over 15 words a minute had a mind that couldn't think fast enough to keep up with his tongue.

Carrabelle gives the appearance of a geared-down, slow-paced town, but when we asked a young man with long hair if there was much to do around Carrabelle, he replied, "It's an action-packed town but you have to turn over a few rocks first."

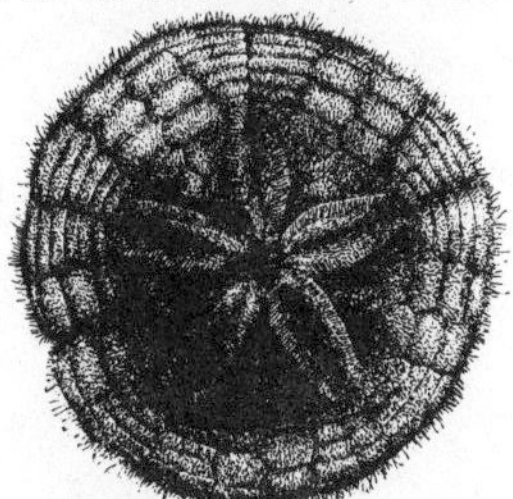

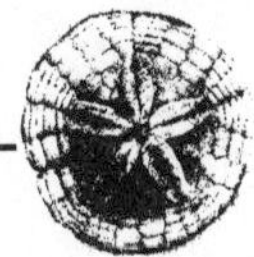

TAMING THE BIG BEND

Chapter 7

If there is one main, underlying factor why the natural cruising attributes of the Florida Panhandle do not attract the attention they seemingly deserve, it could be that not many want to come to terms with a body of land and water known as the Big Bend. Its distance from populous boating centers is the common explanation. While that has to be considered by those with limited cruising time, the overrated specter of the Big Bend itself may well be a companion reason.

How valid is all the pessimistic talk about the Big Bad Bend? There should be some concern when undertaking it, but it all shakes down to selecting the right kind of weather in one or two potential problem months of the year, the ability to pilot and navigate in a reasonable manner and to simply understand the options.

There's a lot of open water, around 160 nautical miles of it, if one wants to go straight from Carrabelle or Apalachicola to Clearwater Beach or Tarpon Springs. Sailboats and fast powerboats do it routinely in acceptable weather.

Another way, longer by about 30 miles, follows the bend of the land and shoals along a course marked by navigational aids. There are two ports of refuge along this route. This is the passage for the uncertain first-timer, those who do not wish to sail or power all day and all night, and others who like to sail nearer land.

The Big Bend navigational aids were put in place in October of 1974, concluding a public campaign by this writer which lasted a little over three years. Prior to that, several lives had been lost along the Big Bend, including six aboard a Coast Guard airplane on a rescue mission. Not all problems were weather-related; some boats had to be towed in when navigational errors resulted in exhausted fuel supplies.

At one point, the project was almost abandoned when the Coast Guard's funds were well below the cost estimated by private marine contractors. The Coast Guard proceeded to place the aids itself.

The seasonal factor is a problem in coping with the Big Bend. When trouble occurs, it generally does so in the late fall or early winter, when traffic is bound mainly to ports in southern Florida or the Bahamas. Our observations here deal largely with those headed south. (In spring, the weather for boats en route to northwest Florida, Mobile, New Orleans and points beyond is generally kind.)

Most of the winter-fleeing flock come down the Mississippi River to New Orleans, then take the protected Gulf Intracoastal Waterway to Apalachicola. There the all-important weather watch starts. If it's good upon arrival, and the long range forecast is promising, some take right off from there. Otherwise, many yachts move on 30 miles to Carrabelle—where it is not uncommon to find boats stacked up on "weather hold" for several days.

Isolated patches of cold winter weather reach down from the Great Lakes to the Florida west coast, hitting particularly the Panhandle, the only area in Florida that admits to having a winter. These windy, cold periods may last three to four days, sometimes so closely spaced that it is too risky to try to outrun the weather system all the way to Clearwater or Tampa Bay. Several years ago, two people in a fast, twin-screw houseboat gambled on that and lost their lives when time ran out.

Anyone who hasn't done his homework for the Big Bend trek, by either the shorter or the longer route, should be prepared to wait, picking up a Carrabelle crash course in nail-biting and weather-cussing while doing so. The frustration of waiting is lessened somewhat by Apalachicola and Carrabelle being nice-people communities with fresh seafood close at hand.

For some cruisers, time runs out waiting for good weather. This can mean either bringing in a new crew or hiring a local captain to take the boat to a west coast port or one in South Florida. Some owners hire a captain to travel with them. Both Apalachicola and Carrabelle have available captains—Cleve Randolph in Apalachicola and Howard Hall and Catfish Jackson in Carrabelle.

It's worth noting they are as wary of the seaworthiness of your boat as you are of their boat-handling ability and Big Bend-crossing experience. A rule of thumb is, if they are still around, still delivering, they must be doing things right, picking good "horses" to ride.

Whether to take the risk, in marginal weather, and how to do it can result in some distracting dockside forums. A weather bureau office is located at the Apalachicola airport; forecasters there are familiar with the Big Bend picture.

Choice of Courses

It may be helpful to consider Big Bend in three or four segments. From Carrabelle to Steinhatchee is about 70 nautical miles, depending upon the starting point. From Steinhatchee to Cedar Key it is roughly 45 miles, but there is merit in adding another 17 to the Withlacoochee River entrance. A fast powerboat can compress the first two legs into one.

There is also the possibility of heading for the St. Marks River, though it is off the route about 10 miles, about 53 miles from Carrabelle. It's valuable as an alternative in case of early engine problems, or if the morning weather doesn't pan out as advertised. In good October weather, it can make a pleasant side trip for those with time to spare.

Steinhatchee often is overlooked as a place to get off the Gulf for a rest or to wait out a spell of inclement weather. The entrance to this small resort and fishing village is easy for the attentive boatman.

Next port down the line from Steinhatchee is Cedar Key. It's a pivotal point on the course in terms of distance, because it is the stop for either the first or second leg—leaving the next good weather day for pushing on to Tarpon Springs or Clearwater.

The first-time Big Bend tripper is probably better off choosing his route before arriving at Apalachicola or Carrabelle. It beats last-minute coin-tossing and confusing local and transient opinions. True, everyone waits on the whim and pleasure of the weather, but research and planning are confidence-builders.

The advantage of the more inshore, marked route is that it provides an arc-shaped course, five to 12 miles from shore in water depths of 18 to 23 feet. The lighted markers average about 12 miles apart. Compare this to the shorter, offshore option that at times puts boat operators as much as 50 miles from land in water over 150 feet deep. In addition, wave action offshore can be more severe in hard going than along the shallow, buoyed course where, according to old-timers, there is a cushioning effect. In deteriorating weather, veterans of the passage know when to change course in order to get smoother going.

The newcomer, caught far out on the shorter course, may be fatigued battling the seas. If a hard westerly prevails, it can mean long hours of rolling in a beam sea or perhaps steering downwind in following seas with all the work that entails. Don't forget it is nearly a 160-mile haul, a major commitment for most cruisers who use their boats only for recreational purposes.

Appalachicola's Captain Cleve Randolph says the best fall month to make the Gulf of Mexico crossing is October. The most troublesome wind direction is from south to west, which usually produces beam seas—uncomfortable for powerboats but not bad for sailboats. Northwest winds, on the other hand, produce stern seas, unpleasant for the long trek even with the slave work of the automatic pilot.

Randolph advises not to go in southerly winds of 15 knots or over. The favored wind direction, he believes, is northeast, which provides the protective lee of land and good sea conditions on the inshore,

marked route. A considerable portion of the Big Bend runs east-west, contrary to the general north-south direction of the Florida peninsula. Capt. Randolph uses the inshore route when weather dictates, and advises newcomers to go that way, too.

Another advantage to the longer, inshore passage is that it gives you a chance to double-check course and compass against the large markers and lights on steel dolphins standing 16 feet above the water. The white lights between Carrabelle and Cedar Key have a normal range of six to seven miles. However, avoid night running unless you are comfortable with it. One of the chief judgmental errors made by the inexperienced is to try to take on the Gulf of Mexico without previously determining and logging any compass error (deviation).

Boat operators from the Great Lakes, or from the Mississippi or its tributaries occasionally encounter navigational setbacks because of inexperience dealing with tidal current factors and wind influence over long periods of time. This is another reason to follow the marked "marine highway" around Big Bend.

The need for an accurate depth finder as companion to the compass is very important. If you maintain a depth watch, any major directional error will show. Make sure you keep track of the markers and their numbers; record elapsed time, estimate time of arrival at the next one, and check the compass heading for it.

The effort to keep track pays off if engine trouble requires a shutdown or even a slowdown. If it becomes necessary to stop, don't drift around aimlessly; get the anchor down. If you are on the offshore route, your anchoring plan should have been established back in the planning stage.

Inshore, check your position based upon your relation to the last marker passed and estimate distance to the next one. If you seek assistance via VHF radio, don't count on a large number of pleasure boats picking up your cry for help—you are not on crowded Long Island Sound on a summer weekend. Bolster yourself with the fact that the Coast Guard has a wide radio range from stations all along the coast. A CB aboard can be a handy radio backup in Big Bend country, which is well populated inshore with crab and net fishermen who use CB almost exclusively; indeed, it is their security network, and you can count on their receivers being on.

What are the benefits of the offshore course, apart from the fact that it's shorter? The professionals use it because to them, time is money. Seasoned sailboat skippers who like plenty of sea room and are not cruising leisurely go that route, also.

An acquaintance of ours uses it frequently for delivery trips, when he picks up trawler yachts in Mobile that have been cargo deck-loaded from Taiwan. He leaves Apalachicola at noon, which gives him a daylight landfall the next day at his objective near Egmont Key at the mouth of Tampa Bay. His course from Apalachicola is 139 degrees. Egmont has a radio beacon, important to remember for those reaching farther down the coast below Clearwater.

In the late spring and summer, the longer daylight hours are a worthy consideration; some skippers lay off Dog Island, near Carrabelle, until late afternoon or early evening. They run all night, saving the daylight hours the following day for the approach to shore.

A possible drawback to nocturnal journeys is that afternoon thunderstorms, so common along the Florida west coast, tend to move out into the Gulf during the night. If you don't like thunder and lightning in the daytime, you could be miserable with nighttime fireworks. At the least, the thunder and lightning is rather impressive, to say nothing of the squally accompanying winds.

The inshore course is not without its critics. A dearth of "good" refuge ports is the principal objection, along with shoals that must be skirted. The area south of Carrabelle/Apalachicola undeniably fails to provide casual port-to-port marina hopping or picturesque anchorages every few miles. The coast is low and marshy, good for duck hunting and fishing. The country is largely undeveloped; but the no-hurry cruising family can make much of it in good weather.

Mystery of *Pirate's Lady*

For a time, the Big Bend was a source of concern that had nothing to do with wind, weather, navigation or distance. Rather, it had to do with disappearing yachts, like the 75-foot *Pirate's Lady*, last seen leaving Apalachicola on January 27, 1977. Veteran captain Tony Latuso and his companion, David Diecidue, were aboard when she disappeared.

A few months earlier, another yacht, the *Flying Dutchman*, disappeared. The combination of the two incidents attracted national publicity, including segments on the CBS *60 Minutes* television show.

From time to time there were reports that *Pirate's Lady* had been sighted in various places, that some superficial changes were made in her profile appearance, that a Cuban captain was aboard with a tough crew that discouraged any questioning.

One of the last to see Captain Latuso was Cleve Randolph, owner of the Rainbow Motel and Marina at Apalachicola. His theory is that *Pirate's Lady* had a recurrence of the engine trouble that had caused her to make an unscheduled stop in Apalachicola, and later, in perhaps trying to make up lost time in rough water, sank. Or, she may have hit an obstruction or suffered some other sudden mishap that occurred so swiftly that Latuso was not able to radio "Mayday."

Pirate's Lady was last seen throwing spray and traveling near top speed in rough waters not far out of Apalachicola, headed for Clearwater.

The popular suspicion was that the $1 million yacht was hijacked, the two men killed.

It is more likely that trying to beat bad weather in the Big Bend produced another tragedy. As for the *Flying Dutchman*, the possibility of her being hijacked was eventually discounted when a boat owner reported weeks later that he had heard a Mayday call from the yacht. He tried to call her back but made no contact. His own boat was taking a beating in the same storm that had overtaken *Flying Dutchman*. He delayed reporting the Mayday because he assumed the matter had been handled by the Coast Guard; after he reached shore, he immediately flew to his home in another state, and it was not until national publicity on the twin disappearances developed that he realized he may have been the only one to hear the distress call.

That same publicity had other after effects. The captains at Apalachicola and Carrabelle suddenly had a rush of boat-delivery business across the Gulf of Mexico. As for Randolph, even some of his old customers elected not to stop at Apalachicola, as though it were some haven for hijackers. But as time went on, things eventually returned to normal.

To finish with Big Bend, some suggestions are offered that may turn a potentially worrisome venture into a pleasant passage in good weather.

- Try for October on Big Bend.
- Study both the offshore and inshore routes.
- Research and decide a course plan.
- Don't be talked into something you doubt.
- Leave word which course you plan to take.
- Check ground tackle to fit your choice of courses.

- Have depth finder in working order.
- Be sure compass is adjusted
- Check fuel filters one more time.
- Top fuel tanks off before leaving.
- Establish radio watch if traveling with other boats.
- Don't "gun jump" an adverse weather forecast.
- Consider your night running experience.
- Know your cruising speed, time made good.
- If forced to stop, anchor and establish position.
- Don't run unfamiliar inlets at night.
- Relax—you'll make it sooner or later.

Ports Along the Bend

Alligator Point

Channel problems have plagued the entrance into the good marina at Alligator Harbor here. "Local knowledge," a much abused term, definitely is needed. The channel is not a problem, however, for outboards and stern drives, or the larger boats who know its latest meanderings. The harbor, formed by a long, narrow spit of land extending westward from Lighthouse Point to Peninsula Point, is at the eastern end of St. George Sound on St. James Island. The 20-mile-long St. James Island is separated from the mainland by three rivers stretching westward all the way to Carrabelle.

Ochlockonee Bay

Located on the west side of Apalachee Bay, Ochlockonee is a workout even for those who like to run a picket line of channel markers. To get up the five-mile-long, one-mile-wide bay requires weaving around oyster beds that produce some switch-backs. A fixed bridge with only 13 feet of clearance prevents large boats from getting into some fine gunkholing sectors here. The trick is to anchor your big boat in the bay, then get in a dinghy—powered, for this trip—and take your pick of appealing river country. The Ochlockonee River is 29 miles long, the Crooked River, 22.

By the way, we have heard it pronounced both ways—Oklaw-koney and Och-lock-ohney. Proponents of each claim the correct pronunciation.

Panacea

A town worth getting to, if you can, located about 11 miles from the St. Marks River Light. The channel leading to the public landing is supposed to be five feet deep but we could not quite reach the landing at low tide, even though *Final Edition*'s draft is only three and one-half feet.

Panacea—aptly named—is a fishing village with a sheltered bay, great sweeping salt marshes and the woodlands of the 65,000-acre St. Marks National Wildlife Refuge bordering it.

An acquaintance of ours tells of being in Panacea once, with the front bumper of her automobile half torn off. At a filling station, where she stopped for repairs, she was told the best way to fix it was to push the car into a tree.

The attendant got in the automobile, eased it up to a pine tree and slowly pushed hard, with the car in low gear. The bumper straightened out. "You've heard of shade tree mechanics," he said, "but in Panacea we are pine tree men." There was no charge for the service rendered.

Shell Point

Five miles west of the St. Marks River entrance is Shell Point, with a marina, yacht basin, docks and restaurant. Follow the channel markers, even though at one point it appears your boat will wind up on a beach. This is a popular place for sailboats, at least those that don't draw more than four or five feet. Summer weekends are crowded in the marina area. It's very well protected.

St. Marks

This is a particularly rewarding town for anyone interested in history. It's also a place to rest up while navigating the Big Bend, and a hurricane refuge. The St. Marks River continues past the town; between there and Newport, a little more than three miles upriver, a storm can be ridden out.

The distance from the river entrance, marked by the 82-foot lighthouse, to the town is eight miles. Three centuries earlier, explorer Hernando de Soto did not have such a huge guide post; in 1539, he hung banners in the trees to mark the opening.

An anchorage near the lighthouse is shown on the chart as Spanish Hole; avoid the oyster bar when approaching it. Tidal current can run through there at a brisk rate but it is a convenient place to be for an early morning start.

The twists and turns of the St. Marks River, as seen on a chart, might discourage some from going up, but all that is required is normal attention to markers. The channel is 12 feet deep, the edges copiously marked. The river is maintained well enough to permit large commercial fishing boats, oil barges and tugs to use it en route to oil terminals and chemical and power plants farther upriver.

St. Marks claims to be the birthplace of the Florida hushpuppy—a mixture of cornmeal, onions, eggs, water or milk, fried in deep fat. Hushpuppies are ranked right up there with grits. Prior knowledge of their existence before entering a restaurant eliminates the probability of being assessed as a rank outsider.

St. Marks is also famous for a seafood restaurant known for years as J. T. Posey's. New owner Bill Helson wisely did not change the name on the big old wooden building, nor dress it up in modern architectural garb. It's a three-minute walk from Shield's Marina, one of two in the town. The other is Lynn's Riverside Marina. Both have been on the scene for years and can render a wide variety of services.

Back in Posey's time, I remember walking into it for the first time to find a spirited game of pool going on. It was mid-afternoon and only a half dozen or so customers were around. We saw some remarkable pool shots while the jukebox rendered, as I recall, "Radio Man from Waco," "Grandma's Whistling At Yuh" and "Ya Gotta Give A Little To Get A Little."

That was in the summer. Oysters were not "in season," which accounted for the sparse attendance. Though biologists in Florida say there is no scientific reason not to, many oyster fans still won't touch them in any month that doesn't have an "r" in it.

The fall and winter months are when Posey's place really comes alive. Oysters are available; mullet and other fish are in prime condition; shrimp are back on the menu, and oysters and practically any kind of fish are offered smoked. Most of the customers come from Tallahassee, the state capital, only 18 miles away.

On weekends, Posey's has a seating problem. To fill in waiting time, customers are invited to shoot a few games of pool. A bit of advice for those who arrive by boat for the first time: don't challenge the local regulars to a game of snooker pool unless you are well above average in skill. Even then you might be picked cleaner than a couple of golden brown smoked mullet.

Among its assortment of distinctions, St. Marks is said to be the second oldest town in Florida. Panfilo de Narvaez arrived in 1528 with 300 men. They later launched the first ships built by Europeans in the New World. De Soto came later but the Spaniards didn't get around to building a fort until 1697. Pirates looted it three years later in a night attack.

A century later, San Marcos (St. Marks) was the headquarters of the King of Florida, a certain William Augustus Bowlegs, a British officer who fled his commission in 1800 and came to America.

In the fashion of Cortez and other adventurers before him, Bowlegs married a maiden who belonged to the Creek Indian tribe, a union that won him the allegiance of 400 local Creeks. Bowlegs used that support to attack and capture Fort San Marcos. The defenders were massacred and Bowlegs proclaimed himself king. After five weeks of his reign, he was off and running. A Spanish flotilla of nine vessels navigated the river and recaptured the fort.

U.S. General Andrew Jackson, however, was unhappy with the way the Spaniards failed to control the Indians and in 1818 ordered the fort attacked and taken over. Two Englishmen who happened to be at the fort were executed on Jackson's order, which nearly triggered a third war with Great Britain. The United States apologized, and a year later, the St. Marks area was ceded to Florida.

But a fight was still to be waged over the fort. During the Civil War, Union Commander William Gibson started upriver in a gunboat to capture it but ran aground, blocking the channel. That gummed things up for Army General John Newton, who had landed down near the lighthouse with 900 men. Newton's mission had been to push on to St. Marks and Newport, destroying Confederate troops and supplies, while Gibson took the forts and commanded the river.

The Confederates were a rather ragged and depleted lot in that area, but with the help of volunteers, 14-year-old boys strong enough to carry a musket and a few already wounded but recuperating soldiers, they stood off Newton's federals. The general was furious, withdrew his troops and took them away to Key West, saying the Navy had not adequately supported the Army. A familiar lament, to be sure, but Gibson's navigation and piloting of the St. Marks had been undeniably faulty.

Today, Fort San Marcos de Apalache is commemorated by a state-owned museum that stands in a pleasant park at the confluence of the St. Marks and Wakulla rivers, a 20-minute walk from Shield's Marina. Pathways wind through the remains of the fortifications.

A visit to nearby Wakulla Springs is also interesting. It is believed to be the largest spring basin in the world, covering four acres and forming the head of the Wakulla River.

Steinhatchee

This is a key refuge or layover port on the Big Bend route. It can be a direct run from Carrabelle or, if the schedule calls for a side trip to St. Marks, an easy next-day cruise on the southward trek.

Lighted marker No. 1, a 30-foot-high navigational aid on a white square pyramidal tower, denotes the entrance to the Steinhatchee River. The channel is not buoyed to starboard; port markers are set back 25 feet to the north of the channel. The Steinhatchee water tower is on a heading of about 075 degrees, practically lined up with

the channel. The towns of Steinhatchee and Jena, opposite each other, are a little more than three miles up from the river mouth.

Marina facilities there depend on the draft of your boat. The marina nearest the drawbridge between Steinhatchee and Jena has water deep enough to handle any cruise boat.

Steinhatchee is a good stop for seafood. Although only about 1,000 people live in the two small communities, there are two good seafood restaurants. The better known and longer established is Cooey's; the other, Jack's. Each is good, each has loyal boosters. Obviously, the local population cannot support two fairly sizable restaurants—the business comes from summer and fall tourists and from fish-hungry customers who come from out of town.

Crabbing is a local industry. The Gulfstream Crab Company's fishermen come back with their load about mid-afternoon, when the crabs are processed and cooked for the next day's market. That's the time to be there. More than 90 percent of the crab meat is shipped north.

The Steinhatchee River has been the scene of some of the greatest sea trout fishing we've ever experienced. (Speckled sea trout are the southern cousins of the weakfish in northern waters.) "Come on up after the second frost on the pumpkin," the late Jesse Richardson used to advise us. The fish come in by the thousands off the Gulf shallows when the water turns cold.

I have seen the trout so thick in the river that commercial fishermen could use handlines rigged with a small sinker and short strip of pork; it saved baiting and reeling time. It was also in Steinhatchee that we fished with one of Florida's best woman guides, Captain Eveta McCoy, whom we called the Reel McCoy. She specialized in trout and redfish (channel bass).

Steinhatchee is not what you'd call a yachting center, but it is a good place to know about when cruising the Big Bend. If you need a bit of help, you'll be among friendly people who are knowledgeable about boats, as is the case with nearly every town where there are commercial fishermen.

Traveling the reverse route, if we decide not to go to St. Marks, and want to make it from Steinhatchee to Carrabelle, it is 73 nautical miles via Duer Channel into St. George Sound. A straight line, point-to-point run for mile after mile provides a good workout for the automatic pilot. In the trip between Steinhatchee Big Bend No. 18 and No. 26 at South Shoal, Iron Mike earns his keep.

On the reverse of it, South Shoal to Steinhatchee, No. 18 is the objective to make initially. It is both handy and critical. However, it should be noted that on a straight-line course from No. 18 to the

Steinhatchee is one of the best ports of refuge in the Big Bend country. The Steinhatchee River divides the small, fishing communities of Jena and Steinhatchee. Good seafood restaurants and a crab-packing plant are visited by experienced cruising people familiar with the area.
Florida Division of Tourism photo

Steinhatchee entrance light, there is a small shoal area that must be avoided.

Boats en route from Cedar Key to Steinhatchee don't have many easily seen land check points. By keeping the depth finder on to take readings and knowing our boat speed, we know when to start looking for the possibilities inshore. Horseshoe Beach channel entrance, 23 miles above Cedar Key, is sometimes hard to pick up. Five miles farther on, Pepperfish Keys provides a better position check. A white sand beach on the northwesternmost key is easily identifiable on a clear day. An anchorage north of that key with three to 10 feet of water is worth investigating. It looks reasonable under favorable wind directions.

In any early morning north run on the Gulf, having to look into the sun as it rises in the east makes seeing inshore landmarks difficult. They are better seen after they have been passed a mile or so. A look back at them can be made without so much interference from the sun's rays.

Cedar Key

Cedar Key is 95 miles north of Tampa Bay, about 17 miles northwest of the Withlacoochee River entrance and 48 nautical miles south of Steinhatchee. Prominent landmarks are an abandoned lighthouse on Seahorse Key (best seen by northbound boats) and Cedar Key's 140-high municipal water tower.

Cruising southward towards Cedar Key, Big Bend lighted marker No. 14 is a helpful locator in making an approach to Northwest Channel, which is the only way in. Even those going beyond Cedar Key without a stopover should go in Northwest, then out via the Main Ship Channel leading south of Seahorse Key. Note that while the red markers and buoys will be to starboard in Northwest channel, they will be portside as you go southward out the ship channel.

As much as any place we know, between Brownsville, Texas, and Eastport, Maine, the Cedar Key markers have to be checked off one by one and the channels kept sorted out in relation to your course. Nothing's easy about Cedar Key from a nautical standpoint, or so it seems.

Cedar Key may be a favorite with people who drive to it but we've never heard cruising people rave about what a great place it is to arrive by boat. The town dock is cussed and discussed. Boats with low freeboard coming in at low tide may have a debarking problem. We have seen people climb on cabin tops in order to be able to make it onto the catwalks. In the absence of dock cleats, you are welcome to tie off to utility poles. The catwalks are principally used by fishermen who keep right on raising and lowering shrimp baits even if you happen to have a boat in one of the slips.

For many who survive the docking drill, however, there is enough charm and good seafood in Cedar Key itself to make the effort worthwhile. The alternatives to not being dockside, or having to leave it due to high winds and a strong current, are not many. We have anchored due south of the pier in a small hole at Atsena Otie Key. Go in on the depth finder. The trick is to find a seven-foot charted spot and set the anchor so your boat winds up inside the current rip. If you miss, surrender slumber to a restless night.

It seems that of all the surviving "quaint" towns left in Florida, Cedar Key gets the most publicity. Cedar Key receives so much attention from bug-eyed big city reporters that the community of 750

Spectacular sunsets on the Florida west coast fronting the Gulf of Mexico reflect a variety of shoreline silhouettes. This one is west of the community of Cedar Key, about 90 miles north of St. Petersburg Beach.
Florida Division of Tourism photo

is not quite what it used to be. Maybe the natives are getting used to being stared at and go along with the tourist routine. On the other hand, Cedar Key isn't exactly the same without Bessie Gibbs.

Ashore, the main street is lined with front-porched houses and overhanging trees. The old Island Hotel is still there, though Bessie Gibbs—one of the most colorful personalities in Cedar Key's history—has passed on. She owned and ran the hotel with an air of authority that dazzled even some of the old residents. There's no telling how many tourists she scared off, or at least subdued. It was the way she ran the hotel bar and restaurant that helped distinguish Cedar Key from other fishing villages and quasi-resort towns. She was once mayor of the city, could swear with the saltiest of sailors and had strong political opinions that she laid on friends and strangers alike.

No one would believe you had been at the Island Hotel if you hadn't

had one of Bessie's seafood dinners accompanied by heart of cabbage palm salad. It consisted of lettuce, shavings of palm heart, dates and mandarins, covered with a dressing that contained pistachio ice cream.

Cedar Key has maintained its weather-beaten look, which to some extent may have something to do with the popularity of the annual April art festival. Some 25,000 people show up, literally dislocating the town, overwhelming the 750 inhabitants. Restaurants have been known to run out of food, and spectacularly long lines form leading to rest rooms. The town water supply dwindles and for a couple of days Cedar Key is out of the real world, as it knows it.

It takes two or three days to clear away the debris and make sure all the far-out, avant-garde artists have left town. The locals don't always think much of some of the displayed art, particularly the subject matter, but it is generally agreed the whole shebang is good for the local economy.

YANKEES, CRACKERS AND SPONGERS

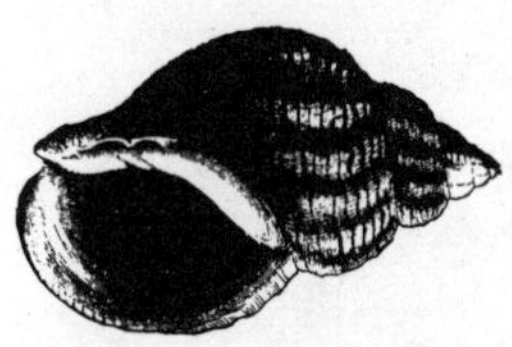

Chapter 8

It's 60 miles from Cedar Key south to the Anclote Keys off Tarpon Springs. Those miles are over shallow Gulf waters where the bottom can be seen most of the time in calm weather periods. Off the course, to the east, there are interesting, even delightful, river trips that can brighten a cruise day.

To miss them, in the interests of making good time, is to deny an opportunity to experience some of Florida's best inland cruising. None of the rivers is long or difficult. It is stop-and-go cruising, in contrast to the much longer runs that are required up in the Big Bend.

The town names are easy—Yankeetown, Homosassa and Crystal River. Conversely, the river names are jaw-breakers of Indian origin. They include the Withlacoochee (Withla-coochee); Chassahowitzka (Chassa-how-itzka) and the Pithlachascotee (Pithla-chas-cotee), mercifully contracted to the 'Cotee. Longtime residents are inclined to call the Chassahowitzka the Chassa-whisky.

Yankeetown, on the Withlacoochee River, Crystal River and Homosassa are populated to a considerable extent by retired people but are not "retirement" communities as such. Each has a large group of residents whose families have lived in the area for years.

Tarpon Springs, the northern terminal of the Intracoastal Waterway on the west coast, has a character and flavor of its own, a tradition and heritage that sets it apart from all other Florida waterfront communities.

Withlacoochee River

Of all the rivers that lead to the Gulf of Mexico—there are 15 of them with varying cruiseable qualities between Apalachicola and Tarpon Springs—the Withlacoochee holds special appeal for us. For one thing, it leads to a little town Peggy and I like; for another, there's considerable bird life along it. There's deep water in the channel, a jungle along one section and, near the river mouth, a classic spread of salt marshes dotted with tropical hardwood hammocks.

From a distance it is not easy to pick up the Withlacoochee entrance, particularly when coming down from Cedar Key. Look for a 34-foot-high white tower but use it only as a reference mark. It is near, but beyond, the channel entrance.

Because the channel entrance to the planned-for, but abandoned, Florida Barge Canal is close by, the area is liberally sprinkled with

assorted navigational aids. The white tower is the only one of that type and helps sort out the clusters of buoys and markers.

Boats cruising from the south to the Withlacoochee River entrance will have to cross the third and most southerly of these well-marked, almost-adjoining channels. This is the much-used and well-maintained Florida Power Corporation channel.

The entrance is 17 miles southeast of Cedar Key. Chart scrutinizers may back off after noting the way the channel winds in and around shoals and oyster bars. Don't let that deter you; the channel is used regularly by large craft. Granted it is a picket thicket of channel markers, but better that than none or too few. Our last count was 43 markers.

Once in the channel, stay between the markers. Attempt no short cuts. Note the direction of the current crossing the channel or coming out of pockets between shoals. Adjust for the current pushing the boat to an edge of the channel. If the wind is blowing, stay upwind as close as possible. It's a hedge against making undue leeway or a sudden motor failure. It also gives you a few seconds to run forward and get the anchor over. The tactics are not peculiar to the Withlacoochee; they are standard for navigating any narrow channel.

It's four miles in through the markers to reach the river mouth, concluding as it does a mild exercise in boat handling and maneuvering judgment. It does lead to better things.

The river entrance cuts through acres of sawgrass standing four to five feet high. The fields of marshland are broken by scattered hammocks. They abound in a large area north of Tarpon Springs, exceeded only by the countless numbers of them in the vast sawgrass plains of the Florida Everglades.

The hammocks, some of them only two or three feet above the level of muck and mud, are miniature jungle islands. The trees are likely to be live oaks, sabal palms and cedars, generally seen growing in cramped communion. Tree branches and palm fronds are often entangled or laced with vines that come crawling up from the underbrush. One or two sabal palms may rise 30 feet, well above the others. There is evidence in the Florida Everglades hammocks, in the form of old stumps and logs, indicating that before the white man arrived with ax and saw, some of the islands in the 'glades were luxurious in tall-tree growth.

In the three fascinating miles of river before Yankeetown is reached, the marshes and hammocks soon give way to a curving corridor lined with lush foliage, cedar trees and gnarled, snaggle-toothed, gaunt old cypress giants, some with huge osprey nests aloft.

Spanish moss hangs from the leafless, lifeless limbs in irregular strands. The cypress stands erect in death with its feet in the water, its grayed and weather-beaten limbs frozen in the grotesque postures of nature's rigor mortis.

Who hasn't wondered at one time or another about the Spanish moss so abundant around southern cruising waters? The name is obviously a misnomer, since it is not found growing in Spain. It's only connection with Spain is thought to be associated with Spanish explorers who found it here and took it home. They also found it in South America.

Officially, it is known as *Tillandsia usneoides* in the family Bromeliaceae, to which the pineapple also belongs. Sabine Ehlers, writing in *Florida Wildlife* magazine, reported there are legends about the moss. One concerns a beautiful princess and her lover who were struck down by a savage foe on their wedding day and buried beneath a large, spreading oak tree. The bride's long, shining hair was cut and hung upon an outstretched limb. With the passing years, the locks turned gray and spread from limb to limb until they covered the tree.

On a still, hot, summer day on the Withlacoochee, especially after a rain, there is a faint whiff of decaying vegetation. Anyone who served in the jungles of the South Pacific in World War II will quickly detect it and the long-forgotten term "jungle rot" will come alive again.

A sailboat skipper easing along with the engine off and moving slowly with a faint breeze and a favoring current, can hear the jungle drip-drying after a shower has passed. The sun might be out, but the unseen droplets behind the wall of greenery fall with the persistence of a shower stall fixture that won't stop dripping.

Going up the Withlacoochee, a couple of miles below Yankeetown, in the late afternoon, particularly after a brief rain, can be a rewarding experience for the aware. The angle of the sun hitting the verdant setting produces a magnification that intensifies everything. Leaves stand out individually. Shafts of sunlight penetrate places where a man cannot find room to put a foot down.

The feathered sentinels, if not the rulers of nearly all that flies above the tea-colored waters of the Withlacoochee, are the ospreys, the fish hawks so often mistaken for bald eagles. The sharp whistle of the osprey, from some lookout high above the river where he can watch for fish or intruders, often is heard before it is seen. The whistle is the forerunner of the beeper alert. The closer the boat approaches, the more repetitive the call, especially if it is near the nest.

The best place to look for the osprey nests after leaving the

For years there has been a large colony of ospreys on the Withlacoochee River between the Gulf of Mexico and the riverside community of Yankeetown. Most are seen mainly on a two-mile stretch of the river, their nests built in lofty forks of dead cypress trees. Ospreys are fish hawks, but are sometimes mistaken for eagles by inexperienced bird-watchers.
Marston photo

marshes is after the second turn to port. We have seen two on the starboard side, two on the port on our river trips. While the number of ospreys visible may vary due to storm damage, or whatever prompts ospreys to move to new locations, the nests continue to be built in the same general area. They won't be far removed from the river. The fish hawks, unlike many humans, are not disposed to put much distance between work and home. We have seen as many as six nests in a one-mile stretch of the river. Whatever may have happened to endangered species elsewhere, the osprey in Florida has multiplied to the point that it is regarded as common in many places.

Yankeetown

Most anytime in Yankeetown is a good time to be there. Spring is extra special. So is fall, when the lethargies of summer have been moved out by the October and November crispness in the air.

We like the tree-lined streets, the sun filtering down through openings in the tree-leafed canopy, the gentle swaying of the Spanish moss, the sight of the river transporting small rafts of water hyacinth which are hitch-hiking with the tidal current.

Yankeetown is small enough to sometimes hear a car coming before you can see it. The tires drumming on the road surface send a rumbling warning to move over. Horns are used only to signal a passing hello to a friend out in a backyard. There is no traffic light to separate the pedestrians and the motorists.

In this town of a scant few hundred, roads go around trees. Cutting a tree down in Yankeetown is the equivalent of cattle rustling somewhere else. On one of our visits, the current raging scandal and mystery concerned some galoot cutting down 10 cedar trees on town land off State Road 40.

The town bulletin board had a notice offering a $100 reward by the mayor for information of conviction value. This was tacked next to another notice giving the address and telephone number of the newly appointed "Avon lady." Yankeetown is small and aims to stay that way.

When we are tied up at Herb Craig's Yankeetown Boat Company docks, I look forward to taking an early morning walk to buy a morning newspaper. It's a 30-minute round trip and an opportunity to watch Yankeetown, in its casual way, raise its curtains to greet another hot summer day. Sometimes, I am joined by the Craig's one-eyed black Labrador retriever. On another morning it may be a three-foot-long, four-legged ball of wool which I take to be a moppish woofer of some English sheepdog ancestry.

The aroma of coffee and bacon wafts through a screen door. The two-toned call of an unseen bobwhite quail in the underbrush is heard in the brief moments when mockingbirds and cardinals cease their competition for attention.

The walk takes us by modest homes, some with front yard magnolias whose thick, large, glossy green leaves seem to have been recently waxed and polished. The pleasant morning trek takes us

along Yankeetown's Riverside Drive, under a cluster of towering, ramrod-straight pines standing aloft and aloof over cedars and live oaks.

The sound of an outboard motor is heard on the Withlacoochee River. Soon a mullet skiff comes around the bend at a lively clip, the outboard motor actually placed far forward in a "well." A thought skips across the mind: how can we call it an outboard motor when it is positioned inboard? There is a practical reason for the motor being where it is. If it were secured to the transom of the boat, it would interfere with hauling in the mullet net. This morning, the net was piled high near the stern. The sun glistened on the monofilament netting and the lone fisherman steered nonchalantly, using a long extension of the normal handle.

The boat's passing distracted our escort dog enough so that it left us and headed for the river bank. Ahead approached something new to the Yankeetown scene since last we were here. A young man and woman—joggers—began to close the gap between us. In the peace and quiet of the new day, their running shoes could be heard thumping on the pavement. It was a sight common to thousands of communities around the nation, yet it was the first time I had ever seen a Yankeetown adult run for anything other than political office.

The couple ran alongside each other in labored unison. What, if anything, we wondered, does one say upon encountering joggers head-on? A smile and a good morning to them will have to do, we decided. Immediately, it was apparent the joggers did not have breath to spare in reciprocal greeting but their heads turned to us as one and nodded as one. We, at least, had made a nodding acquaintance with joggers.

Past Rex and Betty Pulford's Little Skipper Camp we walked, turning left abeam the old Isaac Walton Lodge, on past the parked Florida Forest Service fire truck, then diagonally across the street to the post office where the newspaper racks are lined up.

The walk back starts. I scan page one of the St. Petersburg *Times*. Reading a paper and walking at the same time does not make for straight walking, something police may have overlooked in testing some suspiciously less-than-sober human.

On the way back to *Final Edition*, a woman stopped her automobile to offer a ride back. She'd seen us earlier, she said. Obviously we had passed her surveillance and screening test.

Morning walks in Yankeetown are worth taking. Any place in the South named Yankeetown would be worth raising an eyebrow in wonder, the more so if it had a sister town called Crackertown. Both made headlines and national television, too, in 1960.

When John F. Kennedy and Richard M. Nixon were running for president that year, the two communities took opposite sides. So much early heat was generated, someone decided a straw vote poll might cool things off a bit, sort of get the preferences out in the open.

One early October day, the voting polls were opened for five hours. It was long enough to accommodate the 290 voters that turned out.

Overall, Nixon beat Kennedy 151 to 139, according to *See Yankeetown*, written by Tom Knotts whose family pioneered the development of that town. The name of Orval Faubus, controversial former governor of Arkansas, was also on the ballot. Faubus got only 12 votes. Had they gone to Kennedy, the straw vote would have ended in a tie, leaving Crackertown and Yankeetown deadlocked.

Yankeetown supported Nixon 104 to 87 for Kennedy, but in Crackertown the president-to-be won, 52 to 47. That night, Huntley and Brinkley aired the results on the NBC news. The Associated Press and United Press each devoted over 1,000 words to the event on their wires.

This blush of national attention had hardly disappeared when Elvis Presley showed up for some local scene-shooting for a motion picture to be called *Follow That Dream*. That shook things up all over again.

Prior to all this attention, Yankeetown's only footnote in history was in the records of the U.S. Weather Bureau. In September of 1950, a hurricane stalled in the Gulf of Mexico a few miles west of the entrance to the Withlacoochee River. While dawdling around, deciding where to come ashore, the hurricane dumped 38.7 inches of rain on Yankeetown.

Crystal River

It is both the name of a river and a small but growing city. The river is six miles long, the middle of three rivers along 18 miles of marshy coastline. The Withlacoochee lies to the north, the Homosassa to the south. The mouth of the Crystal River lies 46 miles north of Anclote Keys Light and 23 miles south of Cedar Key.

In addition to being a resort area and a popular residential location, Crystal River is also known on a much larger scale for two reasons. It is the base for a Florida Power Corporation complex, whose 497-foot-high chimney stacks play an important role to boat operators cruising the coast. Going north from Homosassa, it is

important not to steer directly to the stacks because of inshore rocks and shoals. Study a chart, lay a course to the outer buoy, or close to it. Turning too soon towards the river is to court trouble. The second reason is that it is the winter home of a large population of manatees, or sea cows.

Jacques Cousteau and his crew devoted one segment of their internationally famous underwater television series to the manatees assembled in their natural element. The manatees, prominent on the endangered species list, gather in the network of springs in Kings Bay.

An unusual problem sometimes exists in the summer months in this general area. In the Gulf, just offshore from the Crystal and Homosassa rivers, bottom grass tears loose and forms long lines, or rafts. It is a summertime phenomenon, and seemingly has peaks and lows in relation to winds out of certain quarters for several days at a time. In Crystal River itself, Kings Bay is at times a summer "weedsville" but channels are generally kept open.

It is almost impossible to steer around all the concentrations of grass. Our advice is to keep a close check on engine strainers, temperature gauges and overheating alarm systems. Under the worst of conditions, it may be necessary to clear a strainer or stop to reverse the grass that may have become entangled in underwater hull appendages. The grass concentrations in the Gulf shallows do not occur often enough to present a propeller problem to larger boats, but it is prudent to be aware of their presence—what the locals call "the hayfields."

Don't avoid Crystal River in the middle summer months because of the weeds; just be aware. The water is beautiful, the springs a paradise for scuba divers and snorkelers. Special boats cater to diving enthusiasts. There is one large marina at the head of the river. It is not always possible to get a berth but an effort is made to accommodate transients. One can always anchor, break out the dinghy and head for shore or the springs.

Unique here is a fleet of fishing captains who specialize in saltwater trips to the Gulf flats. One of the customs, followed for decades, is to take the morning catch to one of the downriver islands where it is cooked for lunch. It is done also by some of the fishing guides on the Homosassa.

Homosassa River

This is another spring-fed river, worthy of the four-mile trip up from the Gulf entrance if the draft of your boat is not in excess of the mean low depths shown on the chart. There are a couple of three-foot spots at mean low, but we make it up the river on a rising tide.

Take time going up the short, winding river. The channel is marked but there are shallow areas. From anchorages, dinghy trips can be taken to the head of the river where the springs are located. Here, there are motels, fish camps and restaurants. Among tourist attractions there is the "fish bowl" where people can observe a variety of fish under natural conditions. In this instance, it is the humans who enter the glass-windowed tank.

One of the most charming rivers on the Florida west coast is the Homosassa, a spring-fed river that cruising boats of moderate draft can explore, at least in the lower reaches near the Gulf of Mexico. Shallow-draft craft can cruise into such shaded tranquility as shown here.
Florida Division of Tourism photo

Take a dinghy trip between the Homosassa and Crystal Rivers. The rivers all along the coast, from Cedar Key to the Anclote Keys, are excellent for exploring. They are ideal for family cruising because younger members can get into the small-boat world and make close-up discoveries. Some sort of powered propulsion is needed as some of the side trips are longer than one may care to travel while entirely dependent on the "ash breeze."

Among the books carried aboard a cruising boat, a bird book is handy. Florida waters have a tremendous amount of bird life, including an extensive wading bird population—a good opportunity to introduce young people (adults, too, for that matter), to that part of nature.

Our resident authority on the Homosassa River area has long been Duncan MacRae, who operates a bait house and small-boat marina. We have learned from experience that "local knowledge" is not always gospel, oftimes needs translation. Duncan, on the other hand, is a *bona fide* informant from the outset, as the following story will show.

In 1970, a woman who had been scuba diving near the entrance to the Homosassa had become separated from her boat just before dusk. When she came up from one dive she couldn't locate the boat. And those on board couldn't see her. Soon darkness came. A rescue party was formed. MacRae assembled particulars on where she was last seen, then figured wind direction, speed, tidal current and drift factors, to which he added some things he knew from fishing the waters where the woman might be found.

A few hours later, the searchers found the woman. She was exhausted but still afloat. But hours had been cut off the search time. That's what we call real local knowledge.

Chassahowitzka River

This river, about six miles south of the Homosassa, is too chancy to enter with a cruising boat. But that shouldn't stop the serious cruising types from anchoring and going by dinghy. The venture would probably have its rewards in the form of a few hours on an unspoiled river.

A cruising boat that can take six or seven feet of water can anchor in the vicinity of the marker designating the entrance to the Chassahowitzka. We suggest spring and summer mornings as the best exploring times. In the mid-afternoons during the summer, showers often move to the coast after forming inland a few miles away. It is not a long river, so there is plenty of time to explore.

The river flows through a part of the 30,000-acre Chassahowitzka National Wildlife Refuge. (Visitors are welcome at all times; tours can be arranged.) The north end is at the mouth of the Homosassa. While it is dwarfed in acreage by the sprawling St. Marks National Wildlife Refuge that covers three counties, the Chassahowitzka's compactness is ideal for small boat expeditions launched from the anchored cruising boat.

Primarily a refuge for migrating waterfowl and birds, it serves a much wider base than just as one of the most southerly refuges on the Atlantic Flyway. Many of the migrants apparently get to like the place and stay on. Shallow bays throughout the mangrove keys are filled with abundant growths of muskgrass that are utilized extensively by pintails, mallards and black ducks.

Inland from the keys, brackish waters form another system of plant life. The wood duck, among many others, is at home there. Alligators may be seen in the brackish waters of the marsh and upland ponds. Mink and raccoon trails crisscross through the grassy keys. The river has long been one of Florida's best for blue crabs. Bring along a chicken neck or two—fishing is permitted. If you fish in the upper portion, near the spring that forms the head of the river, however, a freshwater fishing license is needed. Florida, at this writing, has no saltwater fishing license requirement. The spring itself is a true, old-fashioned swimming hole, used by generations of Florida families in the Chassahowitzka area.

Marked channels, suitable for shoal draft boats, lead into many residential communities between the Chassahowitzka and the Anclote rivers.

The Anclote Keys provide several popular anchorages, but Tarpon Springs is one port on the Florida west coast that definitely should not be missed.

Tarpon Springs

Just as codfish helped build Gloucester, and whaling did the same for New Bedford, sponge fishing was responsible for the growth of Tarpon Springs.

Because it is small, its waterfront largely concentrated and its Greek heritage highly visible, Tarpon Springs has just enough touch of a Mediterranean atmosphere to make it a one-of-a-kind place.

You can stand on the main waterfront street and see wooden work boats under construction, view hundreds of sponges on display, walk by a coffee shop or two, stop in a small restaurant to try a Greek salad or dine in the Louis Pappas restaurant, one of the largest and best known in the South. A brief walk away is the picturesque St. Nicholas Greek Orthodox Church, widely known for its architecture and icons.

Not far from the waterfront are several homes of 19th-century design and construction. It has been said that carpenters were fiercely competitive, trying to outdo each other in fancy ornamentation. One critic has labeled the hammer and saw warfare "classic examples of carpenter conceits."

The Greek influence dates back to 1905, when sponge divers and seamen were brought from Aegina and other islands to help develop the industry. They brought with them a tradition of Mediterranean sponge diving that went back centuries and also the benefits of improved techniques, including the use of compressed air for helmets and diving suits.

One of the Greek-type fishing boats was shipped to Tarpon Springs, a double-ended, spritsail-rigged vessel of considerable draft. Michel G. Emmanuel of Tampa, in his illustrated *Tarpon Springs Sketchbook*, writes authoritatively of the early days. His father was one of the foremost sponge brokers in the heyday of the industry in Tarpon Springs. As a youth, Michel worked summers with the sponge fleet.

According to Emmanuel, the predominantly light winds of the Gulf led to the installation of gasoline engines shortly before World War I. The change to transom sterns was made at the same time, while sail plans were also modified, to a gaff-headed lug rig.

The Greeks fished extensively, proved to be outstanding merchants and brought fame and prosperity to the community. In the early 1900s, when their skills and knowledge were producing abundant results, the largest sponge market in the world was in Tarpon Springs.

There were then 15 to 20 coffee houses along the waterfront, exclusively a male domain, as are the few remaining today. The men drank coffee, played pinochle and occasionally smoked water pipes. It was a colorful era that suffered through the sponge blights of 1936 and 1946, but whose golden years really ended with the introduction of synthetic sponges.

Ironically, sponges of good quality are still being found, but the market demand is limited. Moreover, fewer men are willing to meet the physical demands of sponge diving. Still, occasional sponge auctions are held in Tarpon Springs.

Years ago, the early "conch" settlers of Key West had found skeletons of sponges cast upon the shore and gathered them, initially for their personal use. Their commercial worth was not realized until about 1850 when a market for them materialized. Until that time, sponges were imported mostly from the Mediterranean.

Key West spongers worked their way up the Florida west coast to a few miles below Tampa Bay. Then, around 1872, turtle hunters from Key West found large quantities of sponges on St. Martin's reef north of Anclote Key, in 15 feet of clear water.

Although the development of the synthetic sponge drastically cut into the demand for natural sponges, a small fleet still operates out of Tarpon Springs, one of Florida's most colorful ports. The tradition of the original Greek spongers is still carried on here, although the sponges now sell only to a specialized market. The sponge drying stage is seen in this picture. Tarpon Springs without sponges on its waterfront would be like Aspen without skiers.
Florida Division of Tourism photo

During the 1890s, nearly 100 sponge boats used the Anclote anchorage, between Anclote Key and the mouth of the Anclote River, before returning loaded to Key West. At least two early America's Cup defenders, *Magic* and *Madeleine*, in their later, less pretentious years worked in the trade.

Years later, when the Tarpon Springs-based fleet began to work northward from St. Martin's, discoveries of more beds were made off the Cedar Keys and in the vicinity of Rock Island north of Steinhatchee. (Sheepswool sponges from Rock Island are still recognized as among the finest natural sponges in the world.)

Florida has had other latter-day America's Cup racers in her waters. The most famous of them all, the schooner *America*, was scuttled in Dunn's Creek on the St. Johns River during the Civil War. She was a blockade runner for the Confederates. When the Union forces were closing in on Jacksonville, the famous schooner was taken 50 miles up the river to the creek. The masts were removed and holes were drilled through the hull. She was later raised and restored by the federal government.

The present Greek community in Tarpon Springs numbers around 2,500. Its religious celebrations on the Feast of the Epiphany in January and at Easter are known throughout the country and bring thousands of visitors each year.

The chief celebrant of the Epiphany ceremony is usually the Greek Orthodox Archbishop of North and South America. The ceremonial climax comes when he throws a cross into the waters of Spring Bayou. The young men of the community dive to retrieve it and receive a blessing from the archbishop.

Tarpon Springs is only three miles up the Anclote River. The channel is well marked and has a controlling depth of six-and-one-half feet. The tall stacks of a power plant provide good landmarks from offshore but are somewhat to the north of the channel entrance. As at Crystal River, the stacks should be used only for general reference.

For years, there was a lack of mooring space in the Tarpon Springs harbor. Holding ground in the harbor was poor, and temporary tie-ups had to be made with sponge boats. Later, near Marker 39, the Port Tarpon Marina was built and did much to ease the problem. It lies on the north side of the river, a taxicab ride or a short dinghy trip to the center of the town. It is a good marina for cruising transients.

Now there is a small, ideally located municipal marina in Tarpon Springs proper. Space is limited, but a few docks are saved for transients. One other space possibly is the dock at the Louis Pappas restaurant. Dinner guests who arrive early enough in the day can sometimes make arrangements to remain overnight as guests.

THE WEST SIDE STORY

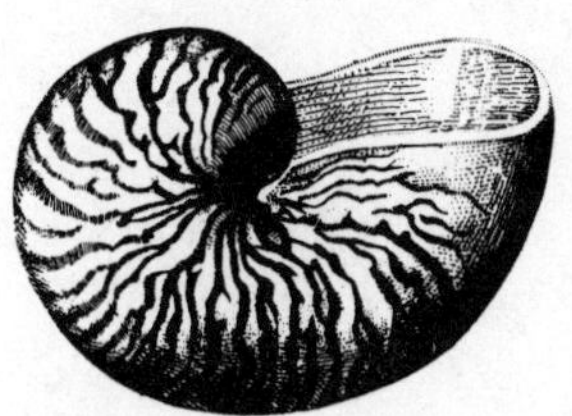

Chapter 9

Traveling the 125 miles from Tarpon Springs to Boca Grande Pass, you become aware of the population core that inhabits the Florida west central coast. The population concentration is not on the grand scale of the Gold Coast, though there are substantial pockets of overcrowding, mainly along the beaches between the Intracoastal Waterway and the Gulf.

West coast development started much later. Conservative roots were already well in place. When tourists came to Florida only for a few days or weeks, local attitudes were not particularly important. Later, thousands of former tourists began to make Florida their retirement home.

The growth rate is now explosive. But nature has provided some compensations. The topography of the 125 miles includes a major-sized bay (Tampa Bay), another elongated bay that is called Charlotte Harbor, plus numerous small bays and rivers, the combination of which guarantees plentiful cruising waters. The indentations tend to provide variety and break the monotony of dense population centers.

The Tarpon Springs-Boca Grande distance can be easily run close to Gulf beaches, staying just far enough off to miss the shoals and bars of passes or inlets.

While the weather exerts some influence in the choice of routes—offshore or inshore—the Intracoastal alternative is more widely used by leisurely cruising boats. There is much to see close at hand; besides, the more varied cruising grounds lie east of the barrier islands.

The ICW has a project depth of nine feet but, in the winter months, the winds are moderate to fresh out of the north to east and exert far more influence than the tidal forces. The water depths then fall below the mean. At other times of the year, strong southerlies do the opposite, filling the bays and waterways above the predicted level.

General advice is: reduce speed. Stay in the center of the channel as much as possible. Don't hug the markers—they are set back from the channel edge.

Anclote Keys

This is one of Florida's most popular anchorages, close enough for small boats to get to, close enough to run home if the weather turns adverse. It is large enough for cruising boats. The chief protection comes from Anclote Key, the largest of a cluster of five keys. A 101-

foot-high lighthouse is on the south end of Anclote, about 13 miles north of Clearwater. On the Gulf side, the key has good shelling, especially after a hard westerly has provided new deposits.

Summer scalloping draws a large number of small boats. If you are a stranger, note where the boats are anchored. Most are likely to be near Bailey's Bluff, just north of the Anclote River, but scallops can also be found near the Anclote Keys.

Many scallopers prefer low tide because it extends the hunting range. The scallops can be seen lying on the grass or in sandy areas. While it is possible to "walk" a dinghy along, picking up one scallop here, one there, the more serious use a diving mask, anchoring in water about chest-high. A snorkel and fins make things easier but are not necessary. An old pillow case, net bag or container is needed to bag your catch.

For anyone who has cruised down from the Panhandle and its interesting challenges, the Anclote anchorage makes a good place to stop. It provides a chance to take stock of what has transpired, to go over charts for the next leg of the trip. Those bound for the Panhandle will want to consider the long-range forecast, anchorage alternatives, and look forward to getting free of the boat traffic lanes.

Southward from Anclote, there's the choice of going down the ICW to Clearwater Beach or out the channel south of Anclote, then down the Gulf to enter at Clearwater Pass. Most head down the Intracoastal.

An interesting stop is Caladesi Island State Park, west of Dunedin. The park contains three miles of crescent-shaped beach on the Gulf, a small mangrove forest, high sandy ridges and groves of oak and pine trees. There is considerable birdlife, plus a 60-foot observation tower. While the docks are used mainly for smaller craft, there is room to anchor and go in by dinghy. The only way to get to the park is by boat, which should tell you something about its being kept in the wild state.

Clearwater Beach

The municipal marina is an important gathering place for cruising yachts. Here, the latest information from the cruising grapevine is freely exchanged. It is the destination for most of those who have made the offshore run from Carrabelle, and the departure point for those heading that way.

It is one of the more convenient waterway stops, thus perhaps too popular. More transient space is needed, but every effort is made to accommodate cruisers. One feature worth noting is that limousine service to and from the marina, timed to coincide with arrivals and departures at Tampa airport, is available. Good to know if crew changes are planned.

It's 25 miles from Clearwater, via the ICW, to Tampa Bay. There are a half-dozen drawbridges, most in the 21- to 25-foot vertical clearance range, but it is nevertheless a popular section of the Intracoastal. To some, it is an interesting inspection-type tour running close to homes, including ours, on the bay side of St. Petersburg Beach.

Tampa Bay

One of the great natural harbors of the world with 300 square miles of water, Tampa Bay is somehow underrated, overlooked or just passed by, at least by those cruising the Intracoastal on a tight time schedule. Not to explore Tampa Bay's cruising opportunities is to miss a key part of the Florida west coast. The 11-mile distance up to St. Petersburg from the spectacular Skyway bridge that spans lower Tampa Bay may be a deterring factor, but the trip is well worth making to one of the finest waterfront cities in the South.

Back in the early 1960s, St. Petersburg began to advertise itself as the Sailing Capital of the South. Today, it is somewhat more accurate to include the hundreds of sailboats in communities just to the north and south of St. Pete as part of the claim.

The bay takes a huge bite out of the Florida west coast. Figure it as 60 miles northwest of Charlotte Harbor, 38 miles from Tarpon Springs, 95 miles south of Cedar Key. The main artery of the bay flows in a northeasterly direction. The width in most of the bay is six to seven miles.

The booming city of Tampa, 27 miles above the Skyway Bridge, is the seventh largest port in the United States in terms of tonnage. For those interested in big port operations, it is a fascinating place, but limited in what it can offer to transient recreational craft in the immediate downtown area.

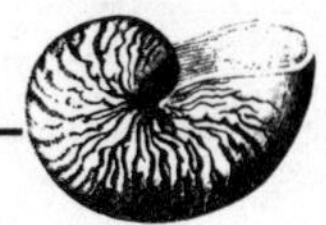

St. Petersburg

Unlike cities that view their waterfront in terms of industrial income, St. Petersburg has a different perspective. Its waterfront has been beautified, used as a showcase.

Several years ago, like many other cities, St. Petersburg had its share of economic woes, due to the dislocation of established downtown business to shopping centers and suburbs.

The comeback started at the waterfront. The city in recent years has purchased over two miles of it in order to control its beautification and usage. One obstacle has been a large motel that occupies one of the most desirable areas on the waterfront.

The city purchased the motel, which is scheduled to be torn down when it has paid for itself. Then, the site will be landscaped, thus removing the last commercial unit directly on the waterfront.

Against a skyline that presents a pleasant mix of new and old business structures, those coming into St. Pete by boat for the first time will readily note two water-related features. One is a long pier, wide enough to permit automobile traffic, that extends into Tampa Bay, with, at the end, an inverted pyramid-shaped building—an instant eye-catcher which fascinates some, appalls others. No one argues its impressive presence. Inside is a seafood restaurant that overlooks the bay and several small stores that cater largely to the tourist trade.

The other feature that quickly attracts attention is the 600-berth municipal marina, divided into north and south sections. The north side includes a long transient dock where visiting cruisers are welcome, rather unusual in a time when most facilities are so crowded with local boats. The city marina does have a space problem in the winter months, so length of stay may have to be limited.

Across the street, between the north and south sections of the marina, is the St. Petersburg Yacht Club, one of the nation's largest and most active.

A green belt of city-groomed lawns borders a good portion of the waterfront. One block behind is a section of one-story shops, restaurants, a major chain hotel, a high-rise condominium complete with bicycle track on the rooftop, a fine arts museum and several other attractive commercial establishments.

The waterfront atmosphere extends back three blocks from the bay, towered over by a multi-storied, combination shopping and

A half-mile off the Intracoastal Waterway, at St. Petersburg Beach, a bayou leads almost to the driveway of the Don Ce Sar Beach Resort Hotel, an impressive landmark for over half a century. The restored hotel sits between the bay and the Gulf of Mexico and is an easily recognized landfall for those returning from offshore waters. Marston photo

professional office center, The Plaza, locally considered a monument to the restoration of the old downtown business section.

St. Pete has other attractions. If you are an offshore sailboat-racing enthusiast, around the first week in February is the time to be present for the starts of two of the Southern Ocean Racing Conference (SORC) races. Spring training baseball games are a ten-minute walk away. The big time show names—and the circus, too—play the large Bayfront Center auditorium on the waterfront. If you like the slower pace, spring through fall is best for that in rejuvenated old St. Pete.

Lower Tampa Bay

Lower Tampa Bay, from St. Petersburg south to Egmont Key on the edge of the Gulf, is probably the most utilized body of water on the west coast. Commercial and recreational boats by the hundreds use

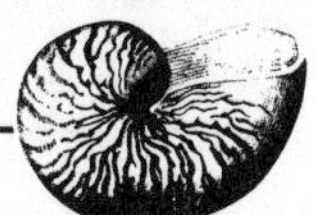

it, fortunately, not all at the same time.

Two major channels enter and leave it; the Intracoastal Waterway crosses it; a cruisable river empties into it. Several marinas and a choice of anchorages are close by.

Egmont Channel, the main one, is used primarily by large vessels. The western end of it is marked by a sea buoy about 13 nautical miles out from Egmont Key, where pilots board or depart ships requiring their services. Pleasure craft use the channel if bound west out of the bay.

Southwest Pass, with a project depth of 16 feet, lies between the south end of Egmont and the north tip of Anna Maria Key. Although not as well marked as the Egmont Channel, it is extensively used by recreational boats and smaller commercial vessels, mainly shrimp boats. Cruising yachts southbound down the Gulf exit the bay via Southwest Pass.

The Intracoastal Waterway cuts diagonally across the bay, a fairly long fetch of water which prompts some to hurry across without stopping to sample some of the superb sailing waters or cruising spots.

Southbound boats on the Intracoastal, coming down from Clearwater, turn eastward at St. Petersburg Beach and cross Boca Ciega Bay to the St. Petersburg channel on Tampa Bay. A north turn there leads to the St. Petersburg waterfront. A 90-degree swing to the south follows the ICW route under the Skyway Bridge to buoys 1-A and 2-A, seven-tenths of a mile west of the bridge.

From there, five miles across the bay, the Intracoastal goes through a dredged channel on a long bar known locally as the Bulkhead. The ICW then winds on down through Sarasota Pass, with attractive Anna Maria Key on the west.

An alternative is to use the channel along the west side of the Sunshine Skyway Causeway. It is well marked, has a project depth of nine feet, and connects with the official ICW just west of the bridge. It is a time and distance saver and also provides good protection when the wind is northeast on the bay. The system of bridges and causeways that cross the bay includes two roadbeds, twin bridges 864 feet long, four smaller bridges and six causeways. The overall distance across is 15 miles.

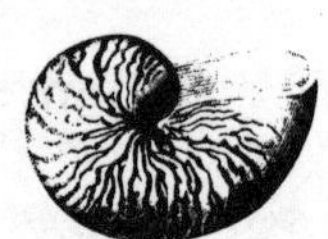

Skyway Bridge

This was once regarded technically as one of North America's largest cantilever bridges, an engineering accomplishment of considerable acclaim.

The Skyway Bridge across lower Tampa Bay is most recently known as the immediate scene of two major marine disasters within a 103-day period in early 1980.

On the moonlit night of January 28, the U. S. Coast Guard buoy tender *Blackthorn*, three minutes after passing under the main span channel, collided with the loaded tanker *Capricorn*. Within four minutes from the time of collision, the *Blackthorn* capsized and went to the bottom near the bridge. Twenty-three lives were lost.

The collision point was between lighted buoys No. 1-A and 2-A, precisely where the Intracoastal Waterway joins on its cross-bay route.

On May 9, the freighter *Summit Venture* crashed into the bridge during a daytime, blinding rain squall, which carried winds up to 50 miles per hour, bringing down more than 1,200 feet of the structure. A passenger bus with 23 aboard, and seven other vehicles plummeted into the bay from heights up to 150 feet. The death toll was 35.

Manatee River

A day or overnight cruise up the Manatee River to Bradenton and Palmetto complements lower Tampa Bay cruising. It's about five miles from the mouth of the river to the municipal marina, and a pleasant trip. Bradenton welcomes boating people; the business community is only three blocks from the marina. Many feel the cruise is worth it just to visit the Bishop Planetarium at the South Florida Museum. The Bradenton Yacht Club on the north side of the river in Palmetto extends courtesies.

A favorite anchorage for many, including weekenders who sail down from St. Petersburg, is the east side of de Soto Point, where it is possible to anchor close to the beach. A few strokes on the dinghy

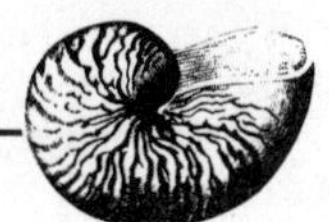

oars puts one ashore near the de Soto National Monument, where the famed explorer is said to have landed.

On the north side of the river, a short distance from de Soto Point, is the Snead Island Boat Works that has been a river landmark for many years. Yachtsman-philanthropist Ned Bishop for many years owned the yard, which was managed by Captain Jim Alderman. Alderman's son, Jimmie, and grandson, Gary, have carried on the family tradition. It is modern in all respects, but still keeps open two marine railways for those who prefer to have their boats hauled on a marine cradle rather than by a hoist. Old-timers called it "being on the hill" when their boat was hauled on the railway.

Egmont Key

This is an excellent island to visit for a day on the beach or exploring. It is a wildlife refuge, but daytime use of the key is permitted.

At the north end there is a Coast Guard-operated lighthouse. The original lighthouse was destroyed by a hurricane in 1848. Near mid-island is the Tampa Bay ship pilots' base with individual small cottages for extended duty periods. A lookout tower there is no longer used because of the range of modern radio communications.

The main attractions on the 1.6-mile island are old fortifications and gun emplacements. The key, named after the Earl of Egmont when it was used by the British for a military reservation, has considerable history associated with it.

Juan Ponce de Leon once careened his ship, *San Cristobal*, on the beach. Hernando de Soto is said to have sent men ashore there to cut hay for his horses. In 1849, a young colonel by the name of Robert E. Lee visited the island to study its military significance. Years later, Teddy Roosevelt and his troops steamed down Tampa Bay, past Egmont en route to Cuba as the Spanish-American war got underway.

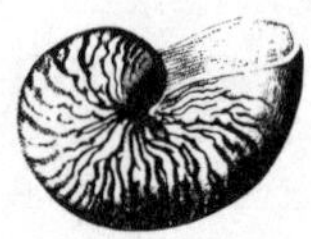

Sarasota

The 15 miles from Anna Maria down the ICW to Sarasota is considered by many sailors to be the most attractive part of the west coast ICW. Anna Maria, long one of our favorite islands and our first home port in Florida, has a beautiful beach on the Gulf side and has managed somehow to keep its development under control.

The Intracoastal weaves through Sarasota Pass on down to Cortez, a commercial fishing village with weather-beaten fish houses and docks. Either side of the ICW, between Anna Maria and Bradenton, there are marked channels leading to marinas.

Longboat Pass feeds crystal Gulf water into the waterway, clearly defining the shoals south of Cortez. The waterway passes Longboat Key for a considerable distance, a key that, with its mangroves, buttonwood trees, high stands of sea grape trees and pines, has become a noted resort area enhanced by a beautiful beach somewhat like that at Anna Maria.

Sarasota Bay, protected from the Gulf by Longboat, has depths of seven to 12 feet in the middle portion. It's a fairly small bay that should be inviting for anyone who wants a break from channel navigating.

Some deep-draft yachts sail down the Gulf from Egmont Key to avoid the ICW, joining it later at New Pass or Big Sarasota Pass. Both passes suffer occasional shifting shoals so common around Florida inlets. Transients should try to get advance information, or contact area boats by radio. There is much traffic in and out of Sarasota and reports of sea conditions are willingly passed along.

Sarasota is highly recommended as a stop-over port. It has a fine marina, many worthwhile local attractions, good restaurants, an attractive waterfront park. It is said there is something for everyone in Sarasota. The Ringling Museum of Art, located on the east side of Sarasota Bay, has been a main attraction since the 1920s.

Adjacent to the Ringling Museum is the colorful Asolo Theatre, built in Asolo, Italy in 1798. It was transported from Italy, piece by piece, after being purchased by the state of Florida in 1949. Each year, February through August, there are performances in it. The circus headquarters, which helped put Sarasota on the map, was relocated in Venice in 1960.

The area has a large colony of artists and writers, particularly on Sarasota's Siesta Key, supporting the claim that Sarasota is the cultural center of the west coast. It also has three yacht clubs whose facilities are opened to those from accredited and reciprocating clubs. They are: Bird Key Y.C., Sarasota Y.C. and The Field Club.

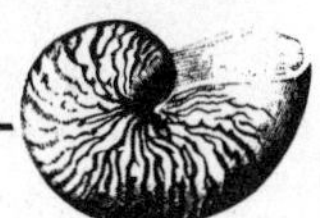

Venice

The pass from the Gulf into Venice is one of the better ones, more dependable than those at Sarasota. About nine feet of water is available most of the time.

From Venice it is about 26 miles to Boca Grande and the mouth of Charlotte Harbor. Lemon Bay, above Englewood, is shallow, but not to the extent the picket line of markers can't be left to reach an anchorage. Off Englewood, on the east side of Lemon Bay and less than two miles north of the bridge, there is a good anchorage area.

Nine miles south of Englewood, just as Placida is left behind, the Intracoastal moves into Gasparilla Sound. Peggy and I look forward to this area because we generally see flocks of white pelicans there. Some are there in the summer months, but in the late fall and early winter the migrants check in from Salt Lake City and the Pacific Northwest to join the local "homesteaders."

The white pelicans are larger than the brown pelican common to Florida, and do not dive for the small fish as the browns do. Their technique is to form a long line, beat their wings and drive the fish into shallow water. They are often seen around spoil banks off the waterway to the east.

The pelicans make a majestic sight in flight, their white wings edged with black, flapping their 90- to 100-inch wingspreads in unison, then changing, almost as one, to synchronized soaring.

Boca Grande: A Special Kind of Place

It is late in the forenoon of an October day in Boca Grande, one of those Florida fall days when the sun and immaculate, cloud-free, blue sky, freshly laundered and dried by the gentle southerly winds off the Gulf of Mexico, are as one overhead.

The alliance of sky and water is dazzling. The blue of the water is a screen through which can be seen the skirts and aprons of white, sandy shoals interspersed with the purple patterns of the grass flats.

Across this cerulean canvas flies a blackhooded laughing gull. It banks, turns into the wind, prepares to land on a piling.

The touchdown is precisely executed, the speed first decreased by lowering of wings deployed as braking flaps. There is a split-second suspension, then a quick vertical drop of no more than an inch or two onto the piling top. The maneuver is completed when the gull has turned to face exactly into the breeze.

A brown pelican on a higher, adjoining piling peers down, as if sighting over bifocals, at the arrival of the gull with its immaculate white breast, gray back feathers and black hood, tailor-made by nature.

The pelican, sadly proportioned in contrast, wobbly legged, its feet as oversized as the shoes of a circus clown, is nonetheless the epitome of postured, measured aloofness.

The orderly scene is shattered when the pelican suddenly turns his huge pouch inside out, its grotesque elasticity astounding.

As if on cue, the gull cries out, laughing. And so do Peggy and I.

Boca Grande is a resort and fishing town on Gasparilla Island, 45 miles south of Sarasota and some 35 miles north of Forth Myers Beach. The Intracoastal Waterway goes right by the east side of the seven-mile-long island.

The turn into Boca Grande is made at lighted marker No. 1 which lies a few yards northwest of ICW marker No. 2. The entrance channel is narrow but well-marked. Depth of water fluctuates somewhat with wind direction, dropping nearly a foot from the mean low of six feet in moderate to fresh winds out of the northeast. Conversely, a piping southerly can add a foot to the average.

When reaching the last marker at the west end, give it a berth of 20 feet or more in turning to port and heading for Miller's Marina. A turn to starboard at the marker leads to a small, but protected, anchorage lined on one side with mangrove trees. Some use it only when Miller's is fully occupied, others because they find it a pleasant little spot.

Miller's marina facility, limited to 14 berths, is full at the height of the season—May through June. It is the only marina in the center of the resort and fishing town. Other than during tarpon season, there generally is room for transient boats, which are always welcome. October and November are our two favorite Boca Grande months but we are happy to be there any time.

Boca Grande is synonymous with tarpon fishing, for which it is world-famous. Almost all of the fishing here takes place at Boca Grande Pass, at the south end of the island, two miles from the entrance to Miller's. It's fascinating to watch, even for non-anglers.

The fishing boats drift with the current over two deep holes in the ship channel that connects the Gulf and Charlotte Harbor. These natural excavations in the rocky bottom, 45 and 75 feet down, are gathering places for the great gamefish tarpon that assemble here in numbers probably not exceeded anywhere else in the world in any similar, narrow, two-mile-long space.

As one watches, the angler's anticipation of a strike is suddenly fulfilled. The rod he clutches bends into a pulsating arc. Seconds later, the line that was once taut, leading straight down to the bottom, begins to change angle and flatten out. The experienced tarpon fisherman knows this is the signal the fish will soon jump.

A 70-pound tarpon, medium-sized by Boca Grande standards, bursts from the surface of the water as if propelled from an underwater springboard. At the top of the jump, four or five feet high, sea water cascades down its silver colored sides. Spray particles glitter in the bright sunlight.

The tarpon, so majestic in its aerial fury and frenzied flight, soon falls awkwardly into the water. But the tarpon has only begun the fight. Within a minute it leaps again, landing closer to the boat this time.

At the zenith of the jump, the tarpon violently shakes its head from side to side in a desperate, instinctive effort to free the hook. Its gills and flaring, blood-red gill rakers create the fleeting impression the throat has been cut by the line's wire leader.

The tarpon falls back, hitting the water broadside with a loud, slapping sound. The tarpon swims to the bottom to rest, to regain strength before again becoming a launched piscatorial Polaris missile.

More tarpon are lost than caught in Boca Grande Pass. Hooking four and getting one is a fair percentage. A guide law is also in effect. Charter guides do not permit a tarpon to be kept unless it is to be used for mounting, or "stuffing," as some old timers still term it. The accepted practice is to keep the tarpon at boatside long enough for a couple of pictures to be taken, after which the tarpon is carefully released.

Ashore, in Boca Grande's spring and early summer, the tranquility of the little community is colorfully presented against a brilliant backdrop of bougainvillea, its red, orange and purple blossoms climbing walls, roofs and trellises. Flame vines spread their network in all directions.

Red tile roofs on white or pink houses peek through the gaps in the foliage. Tall, shaggy-topped palms, like old feather dusters, tower far above the rooflines.

Three short blocks south of the town's center is Banyan Street, where the massive trees are joined in immense, rooted congress, gnarled and heavily muscled, defiantly broad of base, like an Olympic weight lifter positioned to handle his burden.

Above, banyan branches overrun each other, interlocked, forming an archway. Looking westward under the arch is like viewing the openness of the Gulf through a telescope. At the magic moment of sunset, the golden red ball lights up the whole seaward side of Gasparilla Island and the shade beneath the banyans rapidly turns to the darkness of night.

Boca Grande is a "walking" town. It's a little under a mile from Miller's to the Gulf. The walk to the post office and the lone grocery store takes about 15 minutes.

Several large, old estates face the Gulf, "old money" winter homes, not unlike those on Hobe Sound, that are now lived in by grandchildren of the original owners. On Gasparilla Island, there are some smaller winter homes, positioned back from the Gulf or bay, that have been here for 20 or 30 years. In some instances, they are now lived in year-round.

A few clapboard-sided older homes are scattered around town, easily identified by their metal-sheathed roofs and generous overhang of eaves to deflect the sun's rays and speed the runoff of the summer rains. Porches are large and well screened. Occasionally, old cisterns, used at one time as a main source of water storage, are glimpsed behind the buildings.

Boca Grande for decades has been an island winter retreat for the quietly affluent who, for one reason or another, choose not to spend the winters in Palm Beach.

Though its popularity seemed to wane in the late 1950s, the cycle of time has run its course and Boca Grande is back in stride again.

The focal point of the town during the winter and tarpon fishing seasons is the Gasparilla Inn, built in 1910, a three-storied structure that has 130 rooms, 15 cottages, an 18-hole golf course, a swimming pool and tennis courts. The Inn, which is faithfully maintained, has an air of past conservative opulence you can almost reach out and touch.

The hardwood floors shine. Tea is served every afternoon, with the silver and china accessories that seem to lend a touch of appropriate social protocol in the atmosphere of the Inn. Spotless white wicker chairs are in abundance; voices are kept low. Good manners still count at the Gasparilla Inn.

The guest registers of the 1920s reveal the signatures of the socially famous of the era—the Thomas Watsons, the Wanamakers,

Du Ponts, Houghtons, Armours, and top-shelf New Englanders including the Cabots, Lodges, Amorys, Bacons, Saltonstalls and the Crowninshields. Others came from farther afield—Lady Astor, for example, who enlivened conversations with political and social views. J. P. Morgan regularly visited, and in fact, died in one of the Inn's cottages on March 13, 1943. The Boca Grande dateline was read around the world that day, as it was again, many years later on March 2, 1971, when island resident Charles W. Englehard died suddenly.

Englehard, of the vast diamond and gold holdings in South Africa, was said to be the man whose lifestyle influenced the James Bond motion picture character, Goldfinger. Englehard died of a heart attack a few hours after his friend and house guest, former President Lyndon B. Johnson, had departed for his Texas ranch.

Boca Grande is a small town of under 300. It has no school, no barber, no fast food outlet and no cemetary even though it may be fashionable for some to expire in Boca Grande. It doesn't have a hospital, but it has a medical clinic, and one doctor, who came to fish for tarpon and stayed on. The old railroad station, abandoned for years, has been restored and now houses small shops. The old town school that served as such for many years is now a community and recreation center.

The three "Rs" must have been effective there. Jerry Fugate, the local drugstore owner who has met the great, the near-great, and the occasional ingrate over the years, recalls his high school graduation class of 1937. There were only three seniors, all boys. All three finished college.

Small communities everywhere have a sense of humor, and Boca Grande is no exception. Restaurants there have such odd names as Temptation Bar & Grill, Laff-a-Lott, Sheer Folly and the Pink Elephant.

Several years ago, Jerry Fugate's brother, Delmar, decided to build a restaurant, a rather sizable one for such a small town. During the construction period, Del suffered a lot of teasing that the venture would be a "white elephant." Perversely, he named it the Pink Elephant; it was successful for many years but came on hard times. It has been remodeled and is now owned by the Gasparilla Inn proprietors; it is open to the general public.

The Pink's standing in town was demonstrated a few years ago when, after hours, a fire broke out. It had gained considerable headway before firemen arrived, but priorities were quickly established. The package store, bar and restaurant were saved, in that order.

Miller's Marina became a popular Intracoastal Waterway stop in the 1950s when former owner Wyman "Mac" Miller operated it. After a disastrous fire in 1975, Miller never rebuilt. But two years later, Jack Harper, a former college football star who put in a couple of bumpy years with the early Miami Dolphins, took over and rebuilt successfully.

Some of our happiest cruising hours have been spent tied up at Miller's, watching the world around us. We can't remember when there wasn't a colony of ospreys on the little tree-studded peninsula east of Miller's, their family industry the object of much attention. Porpoises cruise in and out of the lagoon. You can hear the cries of the gulls while you watch the phlegmatic pelicans arrive and the mullet skiffs slide quietly by. If there is a mound under the tarpaulin in the low-freeboard, open boats, it indicates a decent catch has been made. Occasionally, a good mound of mullet will be covered with freshly cut palm fronds, referred to by the fishermen as "green ice."

The tide level drops. On a nearby sandbar, a diverse collection of birds gathers, some waders, some paddlers. A great blue heron towers over the rest, haughty in its altitude and high station in life. A snowy egret, so exquisite in its pristineness, catches the eye.

Around dinner time, the mallard ducks come across the lagoon, quacking their approach. We smile in the knowledge that their ancestors were brought down from Tampa in a basket, a gift to a local fisherman who had shared part of his catch one day long ago with a stranger who came by boat.

Mallards like Boca Grande, too. They never fly off to places where the good life is supposed to be even better. True, gnats and mosquitoes can break up the early evening performance, but we'd rather be bitten watching nature's free show in Boca Grande than be stung by paying admission for an inferior feature that came out of a tank somewhere else.

As the decade of the 1980s starts, Boca Grande has its first two banks. Two local newspapers have appeared. Parking is starting to become a problem. Additional lock boxes have been installed at the post office; there is even speculation home delivery of mail might come in the near future.

A new marina at a private club at the north end of Gasparilla Island, the Boca Grande Club, opened. At the south end, the Boca Grande Pass Marina was constructed, geared for small boats, with a tiered boat-storage facility supplementing the launching ramp.

The old railroad station was restored and in the conversion, small shops sprang from within. Private homes and condominiums are under construction.

The town that once amiably slumbered suddenly is finding it difficult to sleep in peace. A few of the old-timers took off for small inland towns but the merchants are thriving as never before. Others dug in to keep Boca Grande, if not as it once was, at least under moderate development control. The line of demarcation looms as that date in time when the first traffic light installation might be proposed.

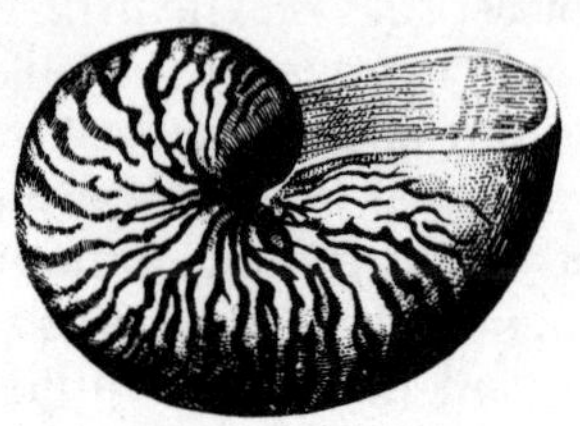

CRUISING IN PIRATE COUNTRY

Chapter 10

Florida once hawked its spurious real estate wares shamelessly. House lots that existed on paper in the insect-infested Lostman's River swamps of the Everglades were sold to far-off city suckers. The lots were peddled on the streets of Miami by quick-buck artists.

Less harmful, or at least less ruthless to starry-eyed potential investors, was the pirate country come-on—buried gold waiting to be dug up on the Forida west coast. Nowhere in the United States was more pirate hokum laid upon the gullible with more salesmanship than around Charlotte Harbor, Boca Grande and Pine Island Sound.

Florida always seems to have more than its full share of incurable romantics. Even a city as large and sophisticated as Tampa celebrates an annual Gasparilla Day invasion. Modern day pirates, all members of the city's business and professional elite, invade Tampa after being towed up the bay in a replica of a pirate ship. The defenders fall back and the pirates take over the city. Tourists come by the thousands to gawk, see a parade, join the fun, eat, drink and be merry.

Though José Gasparilla, née José Gaspar, has rated considerable biographical attention in literature devoted to pirates. there is little to indicate he was more than a figment of the imagination of a fabulous fabricator by the name of Johnny Gomez.

We shall hear more about Johnny as we move down the coast; suffice it to explain here that Gomez claimed that in the early 1800s, while he was a cabin boy on a slave ship, he was captured by "Gaspar," as he was then called. In return for Gaspar's sparing his life, he joined the piratical crew. Even pirates had use for a cabin boy.

Writer Stan Windhorn, in an article published in *The Floridian*, the Sunday magazine section of the St. Petersburg *Times*, on December 26, 1971, riddled the José Gaspar legend. Windhorn branded Gasparilla, as he later "preferred" to be called, a fake. There was not a scintilla of evidence José was for real, Windhorn said.

Too bad, in a way. When we cruised out of Boca Grande Pass, or fished for tarpon there, our mind would sometimes wonder about José's fate. Until Windhorn came along and scotched it all.

As the story goes, however, the day was December 21, 1821; at least, Gomez claimed it was. The pirate Gasparilla had decided to retire. He called the crew together to divide up and bury the gold loot—supposedly worth $30 million.

There was a certain amount of drinking and celebrating. The digging had barely started when José happened to look out beyond the south end of Gasparilla Island and saw a ship approaching, riding deep, obviously well laden.

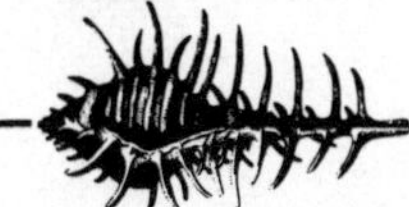

To Gasparilla, it appeared to be a British merchant ship; a nice target, close in, and certainly worth taking in one last foray. Leaving some behind to guard the dig area, including young Johnny Gomez, Gasparilla and his crew boarded their ship and went after the easy prize.

José, greedy to the end, sailed into a trap. The vessel was really the U. S. *Enterprise*, a federal sloop on anti-piracy patrol. Its crew quickly broke out the cannons and soon Gasparilla's ship took a fatal broadside. Shouting he would never be taken alive, José gathered up some anchor chain on the deck, wrapped himself up with it and went over the side.

Well... there really was a U.S. ship called the *Enterprise* and she really was involved in anti-piracy patrol. But she was off the coast of Puerto Rico on December 21, 1821, according to Windhorn's research. Gomez claimed several of the crew followed Gasparilla's example but it is unlikely there was that much extra anchor chain lying around on deck. Only 10 of the pirates were captured and, according to Gomez, they were later hanged in New Orleans. But there are no records to support Gomez's story.

Windhorn maintains there is no known authentic document to suggest José Gaspar (or Gasparilla) ever existed except in imaginary form. Gasparilla and Captiva islands, which it is said he named, appeared, so-named, on charts nearly a century before José reportedly sailed into Charlotte Harbor. The question has been raised: what did he spend 40 years on the Florida Gulf coast for, when the best piratical pickings were 250 or more miles to the south of Boca Grande Pass?

But dead pirates and their legends have lingering effects. It was apparent that John Gomez got around with his stories. Even as late as the 1920s, developers were not above planting rumors that treasures were buried on west coast islands. That's how Treasure Island, a beach community west of St. Petersburg, got its name.

The Charlotte Harbor area was well picked over for buried loot. Even now, once in a great while, someone with modern metal detection gear will show up around Gasparilla Island. So far, no treasure finds have been reported.

However, the pirates knew then what we also know today—that the area around Pine Island Sound, Boca Grande and Charlotte Harbor offers protected waters. For them, it was a place to hide; for us, a place to cruise and, in our way, also do a little hiding.

Although there are many shallow waters in the sound, anchorages close to the beach can be found, requiring only short dinghy trips ashore. Fishing is good and for those who want to sail, there's the

Gulf and Charlotte Harbor.

For hundreds in the Fort Myers region, the Pine Island Sound area is close enough for weekending. From the Tampa Bay area, it is around 75 miles

Charlotte Harbor

Charlotte Harbor is really a bay stretching 20 miles north and south. On an east-west axis it is about 10 miles wide. Despite its size and potential it is still underrated—for years, it was called the "Sleeping Giant"—but is, nevertheless, waiting there, to be used by the more flexible among us in the cruising community. Those who cruised would say, "There's nothing there when you get there." That doesn't apply today.

Two rivers flow into the harbor, the Myakka and the Peace. The Peace enters from the northeast. The town of Punta Gorda lies on the south side, four miles above the river entrance. The Myakka empties into the harbor from the northwest. A depth of nine feet can be carried into the mouth of the river, then five feet for three miles farther.

Experienced fishermen know that the vast amount of fresh water that flows into the harbor is carried down to Boca Grande Pass. It is a fortuitous combination, a fresh-to-saltwater mix that has much to do with the good fishing, oystering, clamming and abundance of bird life. Marine life in and around Charlotte Harbor lives in a naturally balanced environment found only in estuaries that have not been unduly tampered with by man.

In recent years, one government and two privately sponsored projects have helped put an end to the problem of finding boat space along the waterfront. The city boat basin has been overhauled, with 20 slips added along with fueling facilities, a barbecue and picnic areas. The center of town is within easy walking distance. A major improvement was the creation of Fisherman's Village, which has several marina docks, a fueling station and a shopping center.

Punta Gorda, tucked up in the north corner of Charlotte Harbor, was a famed resort town in the early 1900s. Winston Churchill was a visitor and so was that most famous of all New York commodores, William K. Vanderbilt. The real estate collapse and the Depression put Punta Gorda back to sleep, joining a long list of other Florida towns and cities similarly affected.

Today, however, Punta Gorda has benefited by intelligent real estate development. Down the Harbor a large marine enterprise, the Burnt Store Marina, opened in 1979, with long-range plans for 700 slips when its development program is completed. It is located 10 nautical miles across Charlotte Harbor from Boca Grande Pass. While some distance away from Punta Gorda, it serves a large area near the southern end of the harbor.

Perhaps as a result, cruising sailors are just beginning to discover the Harbor and river waters for general sailing. Good breezes prevail about 10 months of the year. July and August are light-air months, also the period when brief but impressive squalls can descend upon the harbor, rivers and all of Pine Island Sound.

For those who have accredited yacht club affiliations, two good clubs at Punta Gorda are the Isles Yacht Club and the Charlotte Harbor Yacht Club. Punta Gorda also has a small sailing club where mutual interest in sailing matters brings people together.

Pine Island Sound

The 21-mile-long sound is the main thoroughfare between Charlotte Harbor at the north end and San Carlos Bay on the south. Boat traffic moves almost exclusively along the Intracoastal Waterway. A long, gun-barrel-straight portion of any marked waterway sometimes can lead you to assume that you cannot safely turn off for a place to anchor. Often, the chart is not examined for anchorage possibilities. Thus, you can cruise down the markers on Pine Island Sound and get the impression that anchoring is out of the question.

There are spots, perhaps not up to the aesthetic surroundings one envisions in armchair anchoring, but they are there. What constitutes a good anchorage is, of course, a matter of opinion. It could be any place where you can get a decent night's sleep after a too-long day plagued by bad weather, engine problems, or a pet sail blowing out. Or, it can be something else.

Three or four times we have turned *Final Edition* off the ICW in Pine Island Sound and put the anchor down in open or exposed areas. In the hot summer months it makes sense and provides comfort to get away from the insects, to pick up a breeze.

I recall one such overnight stop, perhaps two good golf shots away from the Intracoastal, and not far from little Demere Key to the east. It was a quiet night with very little wind.

The morning rises on a new stage. A copper-colored sun, just airborne from the runway of a new cruising day, barely clearing the flat Florida profile of Pine Island to the east, bored a hole through the morning haze. Its fiery ascension was reflected on the mirror of the glazed, calm water. The sun laid down a crimson corridor that stopped a few yards short of *Final Edition.*

Peggy and I stepped on a deck that was covered with dew, a delicious sensation to the bare feet but risky beyond arm's reach of a grab rail. It is a ritual with us to take our binoculars for a 360-degree sweep of the new day.

Our trawler literally dozed in the water behind a slack anchor line. There was not the faintest breeze. The tidal current was nil. Birds were already aloft. Early-rising brown pelicans were diving into schools of baitfish, the sound of their hitting the water startling in the silence.

Three pelicans glided close by, outstretched wings motionless, their ragged wing tips just inches above the water. They banked and slow-turned, at once so ungainly of line, yet so beautiful of function. Minutes later, two pelicans crossed *Final Edition*'s bow, where I was standing. I could hear the faint swish of the wing beat.

It has been written that the pelican's wing rhythm can be slowed to one-and-one-half seconds for one complete cycle of the wing beat. No other big bird possesses such measured deliberation.

A football field's distance away, the placid water was sliced by the dorsal fins of three dolphins, coasting along in shallow water, delaying their natural forward half-roll so long there was the fleeting impression they might be sharks.

Atmospheric conditions provided interesting distortions. To the west, waterfront houses and docks and the island of Captiva itself seemed suspended above the water. A small power boat appeared to speed not so much along the Intracoastal as above it, hydrofoil style.

An anchorage, then, is not always the mandated matter of holding ground, of whether it is possible to sail into a hole in the land, then pull it in after you to insulate your private presence and seal off the rest of the world. There are times when that setting is desirable, sought by most of us who cruise. But there are other times, especially mornings, when it's rewarding to be out in the open as a silent witness to what goes on in someone else's domain.

There seems to be something for nearly everyone on Pine Island Sound. Over 260 bird species visit the islands or are present year-round. The attraction for humans is also strong. Condominiums have more than mere footholds on Sanibel and Captiva. There are fashionable rentals in the resort style as well as less imposing rental units that have had loyal followings for years.

Many consider the marina and condo-rental complex at South Seas Plantation on Captiva as the finest in Florida, perhaps in the South. It is a resort with a plantation atmosphere, but with tennis courts, a golf course, a sailing school, excellent landscaping, and two restaurants. The marina rates among the best and its dockmaster, Don Starr, is one of the top hands in that specialized business.

Below Boca Grande Pass there are two passes that pierce the coastal strip of islands and enter Pine Island Sound. The northernmost is Captiva which divides North Captiva island from Cayo Costa (also known as LaCosta). The other is Redfish.

Captiva Pass is considerably larger in width than Redfish, and normally extends farther into the Gulf. Small boats can be beached, larger ones anchored just off and inside the pass. The north side, actually on Cayo Costa, is the more favored because good anchoring depth runs closer there and the fishing, at times, is excellent.

Redfish is smaller, just north of the South Seas Plantation property. Named after a popular Florida fish, over the years it has also been a good place for snook, pompano and sea trout. The pass divides Captiva from North Captiva.

The pass can be navigated—it's done all the time by small- to medium-sized craft—but it is another of those Florida west coast passes which should be entered only after some knowledge of the current conditions has been obtained. Captain Starr at the South Seas Plantation would be as knowledgeable as anyone on day-to-day changes in conditions.

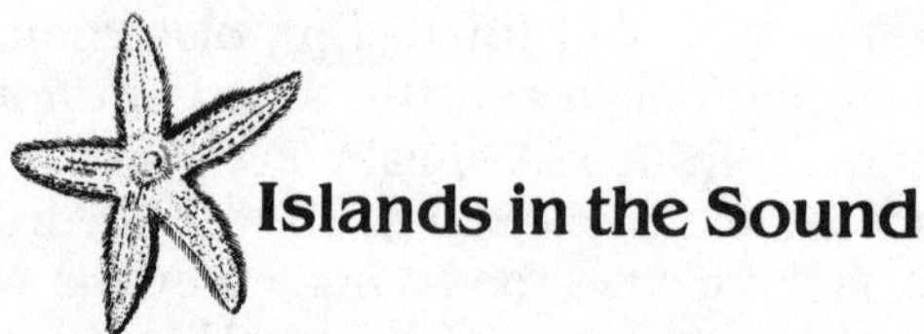

Islands in the Sound

Anyone who cruises Pine Island Sound is going to see miles of mangrove trees, especially on the east side. They are not as numerous as they are below Marco Island and Everglades City, but there are plenty of them. They are far more than what they appear to be—large clumps of green-leaved bushes in a hopeless tangle of trunks, roots and leafy limbs.

Mangroves live on the tropical coasts of America and the west coast of Africa. One theory is that the American mangroves were borne by the Equatorial Current from African sources. That may be the case. These seed bearers were originally land plants that went to sea.

Seedlings that break away from the parent tree float horizontally, sometimes drifting for months, but eventually the root end becomes heavy, causing the seed to then drift vertically. When shallow water is reached, at some point the sharp end meets sand. The shell is broken and the roots spread wide and deep.

It would seem, then, that trees cruise.

Most of the tiny mangrove islands on the sound are uninhabited, though many have names such as Hemp, Joselyn, Cove, Wood and Little Wood Key. Acquaintances of ours, Jimmy and Terry Turner, have lived on and owned some of the larger islands not entirely dominated by mangroves. They have owned Useppa, Cabbage, Patricio and Burgess, among others. Turner buys islands like some people buy peanuts at a baseball game.

Some islands have more of a story to tell or are more accessible to those who seek them out by boat. Our observations about some of them follow.

Cayo Costa

It's six miles long, one mile at the widest point, touches Boca Grande Pass at the north end, Captiva Pass at the south end; it is state- and county-controlled, with preservation its happy destiny.

Part of the Charlotte Harbor area, it has good fishing, very active birdlife areas, protected anchorages, a park with modest cottages, restrooms, picnic tables, and small docks on both sides. The low-key, inexpensive facilities ashore are very popular with small-boat fishing and cruising enthusiasts who have no sleep-aboard facilities.

The gathering place for cruising boats is on the Gulf side, on the north end of the island where a series of shoals rise out of the water with their own little deep water anchorages.

We have anchored there when there was just one half-moon-shaped shoal known as Johnson shoal. But it's plural now. Erosion is almost constant, but while the shoals are shaped and reshaped, they have not disappeared. Getting in is just tricky enough to discourage some boat operators concerned about the shallows.

The shoals are generally crescent- or horseshoe-shaped, providing good protection from most winds. The sandy, shell-mixed bottoms guarantee good holding ground.

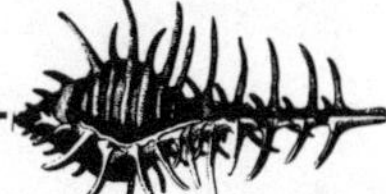

There are north and south entrances but they may vary from time to time. Our last venture in with *Final Edition* was from the south. We found three main shoals and an assortment of sandbars. The south end had the largest anchorage, consequently was the most popular one.

We like to come in when the tide is just starting to flood. Others prefer to enter when there is already maximum water. In "reading" the water, we rely on experience, a faithful depth indicator, a creeping speed and the knowledge that with a single propeller, a stout keel and a skeg we can tolerate a touchdown or a bump on the sand.

The entrance from the north end of Cayo Costa is used by a great many boats, certainly by those who know to leave the ICW in the vicinity of Marker 75 and find the swash channel around the island's tip. But there is a bar that must be cleared. We had no trouble going out from south to north, but did wait until we had about three-quarters of the flood tide to work with.

Northwest winds can make the Gulf side untenable in the winter. That's when to head for Pelican Bay on the east side of Cayo Costa. Entrance is southwest from Marker 72. The north side entry is said to be favored but, once in, the west side has more water. A small anchorage we like is at the southwest end of Punta Blanca. We enter between the land and an old fish house on pilings, keeping close to the island and anchoring off the western tip.

Cayo Costa's appeal is that it is basically raw and primitive behind the beach line. There are a couple of jeep trails for the park rangers but there is no road. The island is host to sea oats, a slash pine forest, live oaks, sabal palms, West Indian thorn scrub, gumbo-limbo trees and joewood.

Nearly all the islands have trees commonly called Australian pines. The name is a misnomer—they belong to the Casuarina family, native to the South Pacific. On some islands they were planted as windbreaks; they are disliked by some folks because they tend to crowd out native species.

It seems incredible to many who have been going to Boca Grande for years that the main town in the island chain was established on Cayo Costa. Several families lived on the north end. There was a power plant, a post office and a few buildings.

The school, however, was on Punta Blanca, a nearby island. The island children were transferred by boat to Punta Blanca, but by 1950 the school was abandoned and students were sent to Boca Grande. The settlement was gradually abandoned. In 1965 only one elderly couple lived there.

Captain Babe Darna, a tarpon guide at Boca Grande, told us about going to school at Punta Blanca and of the old wild horse of Cayo Costa. She was named Mitzi. She had been seen as late as 1972, said Darna, but was impossible to get near. "I don't know how long horses live," Babe remarked to us, "but I've been seeing her off and on for years. She's a wild horse but appeared to be in good condition."

Cabbage Key

Off the Intracoastal south of Cayo Costa, Cabbage Key is a popular gathering place for boat owners. There are docks, a restaurant and an inn. A marked channel leads into the key. Mean low water is five feet.

The main house on the island, now the inn, was constructed in 1938 by the son of the then-famous novelist, Mary Roberts Rinehart. She wrote some of her mystery novels on Cabbage Key, others on Useppa Island to the east where she had a winter residence.

In the mid-1970s, the Cabbage Key restaurant and inn was purchased by Bob and Phyllis Wells, the fifth set of owners we have come to know over a period of 25 years. The Wells, a young couple from North Carolina, visited the island as tourists, fell in love with the property and gave up jobs at High Point, North Carolina, to start a new life.

For years, ospreys have had a nest on top of the water tower. Storms have blown part of it away but, the ospreys seem adept at maintenance work. Bald eagles are also sighted on the key, but apparently have shown no disposition to take over the water tower nest.

Useppa

This is our choice for the most beautiful island in cruisable Florida. Despite construction that began in the late 1970s, a strict architectural rein has been held on the development. Buildings

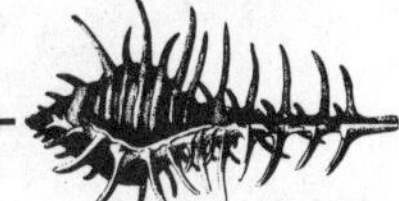

Useppa Island, just south of Boca Grande Pass, is considered by many to be Florida's most beautiful island, initially developed in 1902 by a Chicago street-car magnate. After a series of owners, the 80 acres of rolling property, with lush vegetation and two miles of waterfront, now operates as a private club and island community. The banyan-tree walkway leads by old and new cottages.
Marston photo

conform to the original theme of white painted wooden structures popular in the South in the early 1900s.

Although Useppa is now operated as a private club, its background is perhaps the most interesting of all the islands on Pine Island Sound. Of course, there had to be a pirate connection somewhere.

Our old friend, Jose Gaspar(illa), in plundering galleons, managed to put together a harem of women. He kept all but one on Captiva. The fairest of them all was a beauty named Josepha. He moved her to the most beautiful island in the area and named it for her. But the name was corrupted to Useppa, or so the story goes. If you buy that version, then you have to conclude there was a Jose Gasparilla after all, just as Johnny Gomez insisted.

Usepppa has two miles of waterfront and 80 acres of rolling property covered with lush vegetation. Its alluring tropical qualities caught the eye of John M. Roach along about 1890. Roach, a Chicago streetcar magnate, first saw it from the deck of a steamer en route to Fort Myers. He liked its elevation, its natural beauty and wanted it for his own.

At the time, the U.S. government owned Useppa. It had been selected for a military post and depot during the Seminole Indian Wars of the 1840s. Roach bought the island and by 1902 he had a 20-room inn to accommodate visiting friends. Ten years later the property came into the possession of Barron Collier, a New York millionaire who had accumulated early capital by selling streetcar advertising space—probably on cars owned by Roach.

A promoter who ranked with the best, Collier turned the inn into an exclusive hotel, established the Izaak Walton Club of Useppa (women were barred) and built an elite clientele of socialites. Some of them were anglers fascinated with catching tarpon, then just beginning to be known as a prized gamefish.

Among the fishermen that came were presidents Teddy Roosevelt and Herbert Hoover, and Zane Grey. Hoover and Grey were dedicated fishermen. Their well publicized success in catching tarpon helped Captiva Pass and Boca Grande Pass become known as a world-famous fishing area.

On the east side of Useppa, in a natural channel that ties in with Charlotte Harbor, is one of the best anchorages in all of Pine Island Sound, with Useppa as a beautiful backdrop.

The Captivas

The two islands are a study in contrasts. North Captiva, sometimes referred to as Upper Captiva, is largely unpopulated, except for the north end where there are a few camps and summer homes. There is also a small airstrip. From the middle south to Redfish Pass the island is pretty much as it must have been when the Spanish arrived.

Captiva proper has grown considerably in the last decade, but most people think of it in terms of the South Seas Plantation on the south side of Redfish Pass. The plantation name is no recent promotional gimmick. In 1900, Clarence Chadwick, inventor of the Checkwriter, bought the north end of Sanibel and all of Captiva. Prior to Chadwick's arrival, the only industry was key limes, producing 90 percent of those sent to market.

Chadwick's dream was to make a fortune in copra. One large warehouse was built, plus a half-dozen small houses for the workers.Thousands of coconut palms were planted—unsuccessfully.

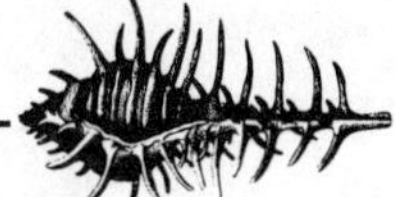

Once a coconut plantation, later a sportfishing headquarters, the South Seas Plantation on Captiva Island, north of Sanibel, is now a famous resort with one of Florida's best known marinas. The old plantation house shown here is now one of the restaurants located between Pine Island Sound and the Gulf of Mexico.
Marston photo

In 1938, Chadwick's relatives converted the commissary into a dining room and opened the cottages to sports fishermen. For a period of 18 years, the plantation was operated strictly as a fishing resort.

But when the causeway was built across San Carlos Bay to Sanibel in 1963. an explosion of people poured onto Sanibel and Captiva. People with interests broader than fishing, and money to support them, came not only to look but to stay.

The community of Captiva has retained some of its old sleepy island charm, though that sometimes depends on one's definition of charm. Like Sanibel, it has been under pressure to develop. At times, it seems that Sanibel and Captiva were discovered by the world overnight and suddenly everyone wants to live there, at least for part of the year.

It wasn't all that many years ago when there were only two automobiles on Captiva, and one road. Andy Rossi, who ran a fish camp for years, had one of the automobiles, and put over 50,000 miles on it without ever leaving the island in the pre-causeway days. At that, Andy and the only other car on Captiva managed to run head-on into each other one night, or so we were told.

Our first stop at Andy's was in 1952. We tied up our boat, *Sea Scribe*, at his dock right next to his little tackle shop and bar. Rossi closed up around 11 o'clock that night, as I recall, but around 3 A.M. reopened it for a party of people he encountered somewhere in his nightly travels. We had the option of joining the party or forgetting about any more sleep.

Captiva has marina facilities and a couple of good places to put the hook down near Roosevelt Channel. A marked channel leads into old Captiva, but go slow; there isn't much margin for error.

Sanibel

Its shelling reputation, worldwide in scope, has made Sanibel the best known of all the islands in Pine Island Sound. So much has been written about Sanibel and the Sanibel "stoop" (from stooping over looking for shells), it would seem the lily cannot stand any more gilding. The shelling pressure eventually led, in the 1970s, to a daily limit on the number of live shells that could be taken.

Unfortunately, the Sanibel Marina, near the south end of the island, does not have much room to spare for transients. We found it to be a most friendly operation, however, and eager to help if at all possible. The marina is squeezed in—or perhaps it is more accurate to say has been surrounded—by condominiums and apartments.

Cruising craft anchor close to shore along the island, above and below the bridge and causeway. The water is clear and the bayside beach good.

Sanibel is 11 miles long, something over two miles wide. For years, long before the causeway, Sanibel and Captiva have been connected by a bridge at Blind Pass. Unlike its sister islands on the sound, Sanibel lies pretty much east and west. We are reminded, in looking at its shape, of a lady's slipper, slightly bent. At the eastern end of Point Ybel stands Sanibel Light, 98 feet above the water.

Slightly less than three degrees above the Tropic of Cancer, 14 feet at its highest elevation, Sanibel for centuries has been a magnetic island, attracting adventurers, farmers, promoters, riffraff, pirates, the poor, the rich and some of the most determined conservationists in the world.

In spite of the crush of people who visit Sanibel, its fragile wildlife is protected to a great extent by the J. N. "Ding" Darling National Wildlife Refuge. The refuge includes about 4,000 acres of tidal flats, mangrove forest, beach, dune and freshwater slough. Darling was a nationally famous cartoonist and conservationist.

The refuge has a bird list that exceeds 260, but there are many other temporary or regular residents, including alligators, raccoons, snakes, turtles, snook, mullet and redfish. Lynn Stone, writing in *Florida Sportsman* magazine, recommends a canoe trip along a marked trail among the spidery prop roots of red mangroves. The trail sneaks through the backwaters of Pine Island Sound and the refuge.

Anogher view of the large refuge can be obtained by renting a bicycle for a spin over a one-way gravel road that runs along a dike that separates salt water from brackish water. From the elevated dike, one can see a large portion of the refuge, do some fishing, just observe the animals or, for the grand view, climb up an observation tower that permits a bird's-eye view of the mangrove forests.

Several years ago, the people pressure was such that, in 1974, residents of Sanibel voted 689 to 394 to incorporate, thus moving out from under the direct influence of Lee County. At one point, Lee County had a planned limit of 90,000; the so-called Sanibel Plan called for a maximum of 7,800 dwelling places located according to environmental capability, setting high-rise limitations, securing setbacks on the frontal dunes and protection for the wetlands.

Sanibel's struggle for balance is a microcosm of the fight between developers and conservationists for a foothold on the waterfronts of Florida.

The best source we know to depict what Sanibel was, and still is in some areas, is the book *Two Islands* by Katherine Scherman, published in 1971 by Little, Brown and Co. It is not solely history, but an in-depth examination of one of the most unusual islands in the United States. The other island subject of her book is Grand Manan, New Brunswick, a bold-cliffed outpost on the Bay of Fundy which we have observed with awe from the flying bridge of *Final Edition.*

Anne Morrow Lindbergh was in Sanibel when she wrote her classic, *Gift From The Sea.* But that was before the causeway was built, before leisure time was within the reach of millions of people, before superhighways and jet airplanes. Her perceptive sensitivity to Sanibel's relationship to the sea and Pine Island Sound is something most concerned citizens of Sanibel strive to maintain.

Pine Island

Much less is written and heard about Pine Island, 13 miles long on the east side of the sound, than many of the other islands. Had its west side been on the Gulf of Mexico, Pine Island would be hailed as one of the great resort islands in the South. That it isn't is because it faces the sound, not the Gulf. Laced with mangrove islands and shallow water right up to its edge, Pine Island has been the base for generations of commercial fishermen.

Probably some of the most serious small boat fishermen, commercial or pleasure-bent, fish out of Pine Island, Little Pine Island, Matlacha, Bokeelia and St. James City. It is a popular place for middle-income retirees and winter tourists, all of whom seem to own at least two fishing rods.

St. James City, at the southern end, was founded by New England settlers in 1885. At one time it was among south Florida's most popular resorts. Some people say Pine Island's time simply has not come but among the long-term islanders, doubtless there are some who don't care if it ever comes. Others say it came and went when St. James City was in its heyday as a resort.

Bokeelia is at the north tip of the island. It is widely used by fishermen, particularly those who fish in lower Charlotte Harbor, Cayo Costa and the Pine Island flats. There are marinas and supplies at Bokeelia but shallow water makes it difficult for larger cruising boats to get in.

Between Bokeelia and Useppa, however, there is good water and anchorages are not difficult to find. The fishing is good and scalloping, at times, is excellent. It is also great dinghy country.

A final thought: developers of the Burnt Store Marina and residential center between Punta Gorda and Matlacha wouldn't have selected the Pine Island area for a multi-million dollar operation if they thought the island's time was never going to come—much less put aside room for 700 boat slips.

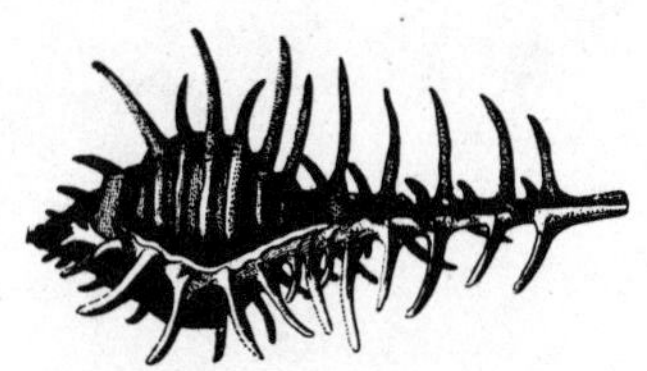

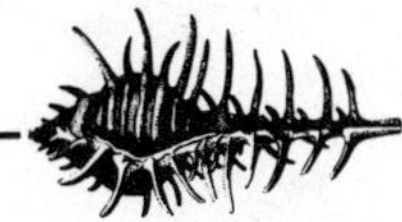

MANGROVE COAST OF OUTLAWS AND HERMITS

Chapter 11

Millions of words and miles of celluloid have been devoted to the old Wild West and how it was won. Much less publicized was the wild lower west coast of Florida, with its share of outlaws, poachers, fugitives, schemers, dreamers—and those harmless escapists called hermits.

In John Wayne's more romantic west, gun slingers in Dodge City and other Colt country counterparts settled accounts out in the open with quick, clean draws. Florida's old wild west was hidden behind a strung-out, almost impenetrable mangrove barrier along the coast. And behind the mangroves lay the swamps. The law, such as it was, did not have much stomach for chasing down killers or bank robbers in the Everglades. It wasn't just the crocodiles, alligators and snakes, it was also the mosquitoes, horseflies and gnats which could torment a man to near-insanity.

Still, there were people who would go forth at night and endure. In later years when alligator poaching became profitable, men developed skins almost as tough as the 'gators they sought. They didn't swat mosquitoes; they just waited until they ganged up, then wiped them off with one long stroke, an arm at a time. They had feet so tough and calloused they could walk barefoot on oyster and clam shells. Horace Roberts, an acquaintance of ours who lived up the coast around Pass-a-Grille, could walk unshod through the devilishly prickly sandspurs. His technique was to scrape them off with a stick. But, then, Horace was different. He could pick up mullet with his bare feet from the bottom of his skiff and flip them into a fish basket.

Then there was Arthur Darwin, a hermit. Even the combination of Everglades nights and insects by the millions could not run him out. Neither could the federal government, when it tried to evict him from Everglades National Park where he lived on Possum Key. He had squatter's rights and wouldn't budge.

Eventually, the government agreed that Darwin, who claimed to be the grand-nephew of Charles Darwin, the evolutionist, could stay, but he was to be the last hermit permitted to remain within the confines of the park.

The Everglades was a good enough dwelling place for John Gomez, creator of José Gaspar(illa), and for the redoubt of Emperor Ed Watson, who killed a few people who got in his way up around Chatham River, where he had a farm. Many other square pegs in society's round circles have slipped behind the green curtain of mangroves.

The distance from Fort Myers Beach to Flamingo, at the foot of the peninsula, is 130 miles, a barren stretch for those accustomed to marina-hopping. Below Naples and Marco, the long beachlines are gone. To travel inland, you have to have special knowledge—know where to go and what to look for. But you can cruise, in a limited way, to the old haunts of Gomez, Watson, the plume hunters, poachers, to Everglades City and Chokoloskee, where the old colorful characters gathered in good and bad times.

Naples

Naples, 33 miles south of Fort Myers Beach, is an attractive city with an appealing waterfront, an impression reinforced by the number of expensive, well-groomed homes, particularly in the Port Royal area near Gordon Pass that connects with the Gulf.

There is no inside route from Fort Myers Beach to Naples, but outside presents no real problem except for brief periods in the winter when a northwest front moves down the Gulf. It is possible to cruise down along the beaches close to shore; make sure you are far enough out to clear entrances to passes.

There's a shortage of dock space in Naples. Unless you have access to yacht clubs—Naples has two within sight of each other—it comes down to finding a berth at the municipal marina. The problem eases in the spring.

This is a community of considerable wealth, good restaurants and fashionable shops. There are numerous golf courses and condominiums. Some view it as a mini Palm Beach.

Yet, only six miles down the waterway, about halfway from Naples to Marco, there is a delightful small anchorage, in Rookery Bay, a 5,000-acre refuge for birds which humans are permitted to share. Fishing is allowed, but it is not the place for water skiing or beach parties. Firearms and hunting are not permitted.

The bay is on the east side of the waterway; enter between Markers 49 and 50. A word about the waterway: it is not part of the Intracoastal; don't count on more than four feet of water at low tide. If four feet is marginal for your boat, try it on a rising tide.

A dinghy is needed if exploring is planned. The rookery consists of mangrove islands, upland pines and marshes. Peggy and I came in one late fall day, planning only an overnight stop. We remained three days, catching trout and redfish and thoroughly enjoying ourselves on our first visit there.

Between Marco and Naples we seldom fail to see a bald eagle, usually nearer the Naples end, and from time to time we see roseate spoonbills.

There are two routes from Naples south to Marco; one is out Gordon Pass at Naples, then down the outside to Capri Pass leading into Marco. The other is down the inside waterway.

Marco

Only a few years ago, this was a fishing village, a snook fisherman's paradise, providing you were willing to suffer gnats and mosquitoes. Today, Marco is entirely geared to resort living, complete with an airstrip and a major convention hotel. The fight for development has led to several court battles.

The Marco beach is one of the best in Florida, with fine shelling. Marina facilities are good; the Marco River Marina can handle boats up to 65 feet and is a clearing house for information, transmitted by radio whether one is a customer or not.

The waterway southward calls for a word of warning. Just beyond the high level bridge at Marco, a shallow flat almost lines up with the center span. The chart will indicate a need to turn to starboard in order to miss the shoal.

Goodland

Not much here for just plain cruising people. The emphasis is on fishing. For us, Goodland holds many pleasant memories of fishing for snook and redfish with Captain "Silent John" Stephens, and meeting a remarkale woman named Emma Hudson, who was 93 when we talked with her in 1972. At that time, she still rowed two to four miles three times a week to catch fish.

Mrs. Hudson was born on a boat, outlived four husbands, one of whom she discarded because "He didn't appreciate a good woman, so I got rid of him. That's the way to do." She had one outboard motor for her boat but she outlasted it, too, went back to rowing and would not change back to power again.

Her grandfather was Captain W. T. Collier, who was the first man to settle on Marco and is generally credited with being the founder. Mrs. Hudson recalled that when she was a young girl at Marco, the island was crowded with wildlife. She remembered eating roseate spoonbills, a paralyzing thought to today's conservationists. "They ate real good," she said.

Goodland does not have much in the way of marina facilities, but it does have several anchorages that are obvious from even a casual look at the chart. When leaving Coon Key, go slowly because of shallow water. Try to time your departure for high tide. Even with less than four feet of draft, *Final Edition* usually churns up a trail of clouded water on leaving the key.

From Coon Key down the coast to Indian Key, which is at the entrance to the marked channel that leads to Everglades City, there are several openings in the mangroves, some inviting exploration. We tried a couple on a 1979 cruise and got a fair distance up the channel before retreating. The charted depths were accurate.

About six miles north of Indian Key is Panther Key, for many years the home of the famous Johnny Gomez. We have found good anchorages there.

Noted Florida historian Charlton Tebeau has written about Gomez in his excellent book, *Man in the Everglades*, recommended reading for anyone interested in that part of Florida. One incident he tells about Gomez involves Kenneth Ransom of St. Joseph, Michigan, and three young companions who stopped at Panther in 1898, in search of water. They arrived in a yawl they had sailed down the Mississippi River.

Gomez warmly greeted his visitors, telling them he was 123 years old. His wife, reportedly, appeared much younger. Another time, Gomez had said he was born in 1778, which would have made him 120 at the time of Ransom's visit. The cruisers took pictures of John and his wife in front of a thatched shack. They said he appeared keen of mind and vigorous. If Gomez had really experienced all he claimed to have, he had to be well over 100. He said, among other things, he had served with Napoleon Bonaparte, been involved in the Battle of Okeechobee in the Seminole War of 1837, been a cabin boy and pirate for Gasparilla, and done a bit of blockade running in the Civil War; you have to wonder if John Gomez was more than one person.

There is an indication Gomez lived on Panther Key as early as 1876, at the time well supplied with money. But a year later, he had little left. He left the island for a few weeks and came back with replenished funds. Rumors spread, perhaps accelerated by wily John, that Gomez knew where treasure was hidden and thus could refinance himself as needed.

On July 22, 1900, the body of John Gomez, was found tangled in a fishing net behind his rowboat, a short distance from Panther Key. The western end of Panther Key is called Gomez Point on most charts. It seems the very least recognition due him. He was a fabulous "anything" you might want to call him.

The Saga of Ed Watson

Gomez, however, was not nearly as well known as Ed Watson, who had a very successful farm on Chatham Bend, a few miles south of Chokoloskee Island. Watson, also known as Emperor Ed, had established himself there on a 40-acre shell mound where he grew sugar cane, made syrup in large quantities, and produced vegetables for the Key West-New York markets. By all accounts, he was industrious and a good businessman.

He also became the best known, most talked about, most feared white man who lived in what is now the western part of Everglades National Park. It was not his farming prowess that gained him recognition.

Rather, he had arrived in Chokoloskee with a reputation for having murdered a few people, one of them a woman. He also brought a fierce temper to match his reputation.

Much has been written about Watson's criminal background. Apparently, when he was still a young man, he killed a black man. Ed had been careless in planting peas on his father's farm and, the story goes, he killed the man for fear he would inform his father. Young Watson fled to Texas where he met the notorious outlaw Belle Starr. He had quickly moved into fast company.

He then shot and killed her. The motive most often given was that he thought she was leading him into an ambush.

He next appeared in Oregon. There, someone fired a shotgun blast through an open window while he slept—and missed. The aim was high. Next morning, Watson went to town, found the man and summarily killed him. Later, Watson turned up in Arcadia, Florida, where he gunned down a man named Quinn Bass.

Finally, Ed settled in Chokoloskee where he bought a farm, a venture so successful that at one time, two of his own schooners transported products to Key West.

Smallwood's store on Chokoloskee Island near the northwest edge of Everglades National Park is the last local vestige of another era, when traders, outlaws, poachers and plain hard-working people lived on and around what was basically a huge deposit of shells discarded by Indians. The building, the scene of the shooting of Emperor Ed Watson, was originally a trading post. It later became a combination general store and post office; although the post office has been closed, the general store is still open. Marston photo

Apparently, his hired hands were not always top grade. Among them were drifters who had heard about Watson and gone to him for help, and outlaws who wanted to spend time out of the public view, for which Chatham Bend was ideally suited. Rumors circulated that he had disposed of one or two workers who had tried to take advantage of him; he began to be blamed for murders he didn't commit.

In 1910, an especially unsavory group, five men and one woman, appeared at Watson's farm. One day, when Watson and another man had gone to Chokoloskee, a man named Cox killed the woman and two of the men.

When Watson returned, he killed Cox. He later went back to Chokoloskee to buy shotgun shells at Charles B. Smallwood's store; Emperor Ed brought a cap which he claimed was evidence that he had killed Cox. A crowd gathered, wanting to see Cox's body. It was agreed that Watson would lead them to his farm; upon being told he could not take his shotgun along, his famous temper flared. Ed put his shotgun to his shoulder but it failed to fire—it was later found the shells purchased were wet—he then grabbed for his six-shooter, but it was too late. The crowd began to fire, and Emperor Watson fell dead.

Afterwards, it was commonly agreed most everyone fired because they were mortally afraid of Watson. The 1946 edition of the WPA *Florida Guide* carried this comment: "Witnesses declared that he was buried in a shallow trench, with an end of a rope running from the grave and tied to a tree, signifying shooting was too good for him."

Tebeau's *Man in the Everglades* does not mention the rope. It simply states neighbors of Watson buried him on nearby Rabbit Key. His body was removed several days later and buried at Fort Myers where his wife's family lived.

Those who had business dealings with him said he paid his bills and was friendly. Charles "Ted" Smallwood always defended Watson as far as his dealings with him were concerned. In December of 1972, I talked with Thelma Smallwood, the captain's daughter.

She had taken over the store, which was also the local post office at that time. Inevitably, Watson's name came up. She remarked rather coolly, "Seems that's all some people want to talk about when they come here." Watson had died 62 years earlier and Thelma thought it was time to talk about something else in Chokoloskee. Though it's no longer the post office, the store is open for a few hours each day. With the passing of Thelma Smallwood, the store will be left to the state as an historic landmark.

Hurricane Donna in 1960 blew away most of Ed Watson's farm, but not his legend. There really was an old Wild West on the west coast of Florida.

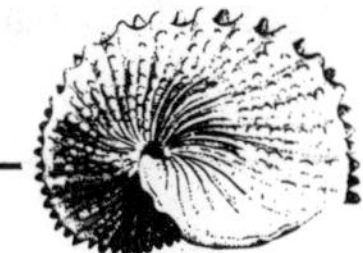

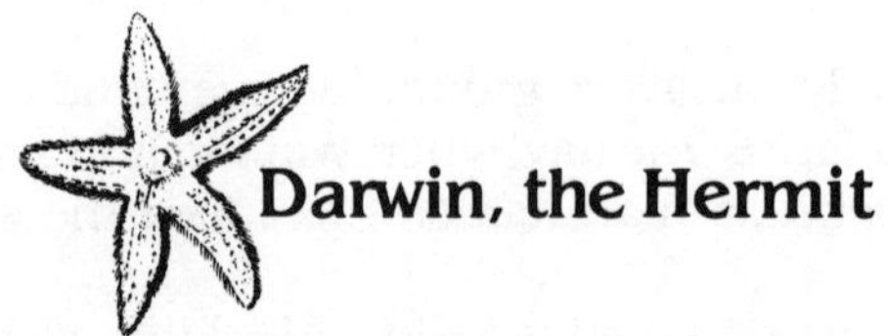

Darwin, the Hermit

Arthur Leslie Darwin was no ordinary man. No ordinary man could have lived for 27 years on a little island in the Florida Everglades under conditions that would have driven many another person mad. A few days might be tolerable, but not the nights. Or is it that we are so fine-tuned to our sophisticated, technological society, that we cannot long endure discomfort, isolation and deprivation?

People who met him—he made periodic trips to Chokoloskee and Everglades City—were fascinated with his claims to kinship to Charles Darwin. Otherwise he would have been just another hermit in need of a bath. His was an interesting history.

He was born in Arkansas on December 10, 1879, fathered nine children and headed for Florida in 1934 to avoid taking a Work Progress Administration (WPA) job.

Possum Key, where Darwin lived, is in a narrow creek between Chevalier and Cannon bays, at Marker 87 on the Wilderness Waterway, a 100-mile through-the-islands water route from Everglades City to Flamingo on Florida Bay. The inside passage was used by Indians and fishing guides but there were no charts until 1969, when the markers were put in. Only small, low-profile boats can navigate the trail today.

The University of Miami's *Guide to the Wilderness Waterway,* written by park naturalist William Truesdell, lists Darwin's camp on the waterway as one of the "must" things to see.

Calusa Indians had lived on Possum Key and in the area for hundreds of years before the Spanish explorers appeared. They ate shellfish, extremely plentiful in that era, and dumped shells wherever they ate. Possum Key grew in size as the shells piled up until it became five acres in size and rose a half-dozen feet above the water.

Possum was not the only shell mound in the area. Indeed, Chokoloskee Island, next to Everglades City, is an Indian shell mound. It is the largest in that area—with 144 acres and a top elevation of 27 feet.

Darwin started his Florida life down at Lostman's River before it was part of Everglades National Park. He was trapping there by 1935, concentrating on otter and raccoon. For eight years, he was in that area, alligator hunting in the summer months.

In 1942 he moved to the mainland to build boats at Chokoloskee and Everglades City. His ability as a carpenter was to come in handy after he moved out to Possum Key in 1945. He started with a tent, but gradually expanded.

From Pavillion Key he brought sand, from Everglades City he got cement. Shell was plentiful on Possum. He built a one-room camp of concrete blocks. A cistern was constructed to catch rainwater. He started planting 350 banana trees.

In periods of drought, salt water intrusion became a problem. In the end, he feels, altering the natural flow of water from the Everglades "river of grass" killed all vegetable life on Possum Key.

Although he lived alone, he was not averse to having company, especially fishermen stopping by with beer, or even stronger stuff. As a matter of fact, Darwin had a still that produced yellow corn whisky that was about 100 proof. It went down easy, they say, coming out of a five-gallon jug, but there might have been bits of charcoal in it.

In 1953, when the federal government tried to evict Arthur from the Park, he came up with a classic case of squatter's rights.

He demanded $45,000 for his banana trees, guavas, limes, coconuts, assorted vegetables, house and cistern. Washington had some second thoughts. Three years later, Darwin went to Miami and signed a quit-claim deed in federal court in return for the right to live out his natural life on the key.

Many are the stories about Darwin, "Only about half of them are true," he said with a smile. I asked him about the veracity of the story he was bitten by a cottonmouth snake. Was it true that he "walked it off?"

"Yes, sir, I did. Got me way up in the thigh. I put a bottle of whisky on the table and started walking. Kept it up for hours, stopping by every few minutes for some of the whisky. Eventually the pain went away. A doctor later told me I did right. There's no serum for a cottonmouth bite, or wasn't at that time."

I last saw Arthur Leslie Darwin, last man to legally live in Everglades National Park, in late November of 1972. I found him on a houseboat—more of a camp—in Everglades City. He was well out of the element he loved so much. Although he was starting to fail in health, what had prompted him to leave Possum was the loss of his banana plants, guavas and other things he grew as part of his survival plan.

"I must have gone crazy out there," he said as he stood in the doorway of the houseboat. "Tannic acid ruined everything. It's all gone. Nothing's left. Now I don't feel well. The doctors don't seem to be able to do much for me."

He was once asked if he was afraid to die alone out on Possum Key. "No, I deal direct with Jesus Christ," he said. "I've got the book that tells all about it. It's just between Him and me." Darwin died in his late 90s.

Everglades City

Peggy and I have always enjoyed Everglades City, a commercial fishing port with an assortment of workboats adapted for the crab, pompano and mackerel markets. Occasionally, manatees, moving along with the tide, have come close by our boat berthed at the lodge marina.

In terms of mileage, this is a natural stopover for those cruising between Naples and the Florida Keys, or taking shorter hitches, such as a leg over to Shark River. It's 33 miles above the Little Shark River entrance, 55 from Flamingo.

There are good anchorages just off the Gulf near Indian Key. The distance to Everglades City is only six miles over a marked channel.

The Everglades Rod and Gun Club Lodge has been a landmark on the river for decades. It has a long seawall-type marina that can handle several large yachts. The lodge has a restaurant and a screened-in swimming pool.

Everglades City was once the seat of the Collier County government, but eventually lost it to Naples. Hurricane Donna delivered a severe blow to many homes in the little community when the storm tide spilled over the banks of the Barron River.

When we first cruised there in the early 1950s, the Barron Collier interests still were in charge, but development plans were stalling out. On one corner of the main street there was a building in which movies were shown. A portion of it was opened on the sides but screened in. The mosquito fogging truck would come by sometime during the showing and "bomb" the spectators. Locals told us the Seminole Indians used to come into town Saturday nights and "boo" the Hollywood "Indians" in the shoot-and-scalp sagas.

Everglades City has been the shooting scene of three or four motion pictures, none of them award-winners but bringing into the lodge over the years such name characters as Gypsy Rose Lee, Burl Ives, Chuck Connors, and David Carradine.

Chokoloskee

This is a key place for small-boat fishermen and headquarters for snook, redfish and tarpon guides, though there are also several guides that work out of Everglades City. Smallwood's store passes as the main tourist attraction.

Chokoloskee is only a half-mile wide and really is one great shell mound. Unless you are going over to fish, there isn't a great deal to see, but in the context of its rugged past, the ability of the little island to survive the worst of hurricanes and the best and worst of men who have sought it out, it's worth the trip.

There is a causeway from Everglades City but it is more fun to go over by dinghy. The channel is marked and runs past one of the national park buildings where arrangements can be made for a bird-watching trip.

Shark River Country

To many who cruise the lower Florida west coast, Shark River is synonymous with Everglades National Park. Newcomers tend to regard it with apprehension.

Getting to the Shark River entrance from October through May, either coming up to it from the Florida Keys or down from Everglades City, presents a small but noteworthy problem. There are hundreds, if not thousands, of stone-crab trap buoys strung together in long lines.

In general, try to run parallel and to leeward of the buoys. Observe the buoys to determine the tidal current or wind set. They are tethered to a long line attached to the even longer main line that connects all the traps. Noting the wind or current effect also gives you a clue to possible navigational corrections on the compass course heading.

There are two Shark rivers: Little Shark where the entrance marker is located, and Shark River. The latter is north of Little Shark,

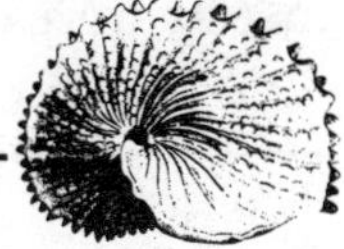

but the two join seven miles inland. Shark River can be cruised for several miles in water six feet deep. We have taken *Final Edition* the 12 miles to Tarpon Bay without incident, although jutting oyster bars have to be avoided. The chart of the river is accurate but should be checked closely while en route for the proper turns.

If you appreciate a sensation of isolation, Tarpon Bay is the place to experience it and set up a dinghy base. You'll live in a broad circle of mangroves, on a protected bay with scores of creeks and at least one large river to explore.

Peggy and I once anchored there for five days. We had company—actually, notable visitors who came via television. The only station we could reach, Miami's Channel 6, came in beautifully. Its programming of old movies was unique, and that particular week it ran a whole string of Bette Davis movies. Little flashbacks of memories brighten the recollections of a cruise and establish specific identities with a certain place. When we think of Tarpon Bay, we also think of Bette Davis.

Harney River, leading from Tarpon Bay, looked particularly inviting for a small boat excursion, which we regret not attempting. Harney empties into the Gulf. We did do some dinghy-exploring in another area and in a creek saw the first crocodile Peggy and I had ever seen in Florida.

River and creek trips in the Everglades should not be attempted without a chart. Possible points of confusion should be noted on the chart for the return trip. Also aboard the dinghy should be a compass, extra shear pins for the outboard motor, a paddle or two and extra drinking water. If lost, one could follow an ebbing current to the Gulf but it might leave you miles from where you started or wanted to be.

The time *not* to be in Shark River country is after late March or April. Hordes of insects dominate. No insect repellent should be marketed without field trials in Shark River and most of the Everglades. In the summer months, no area below Venice is bug-proof without aerial spraying and other counter-measures. They diminish but do not eliminate.

It seems incredible today to those who cruise into Shark River that there was a mangrove bark company operating on the river in 1908. The plan was to extract tannic acid from the bark and use the rest for good quality hardwood lumber. The Shark River site was selected after the mangroves began to disappear on an island strip that became known as Miami Beach!

The hurricane of 1910 destroyed the factory on Shark River. The insects were cruel to the workers. One man recalls the sight of men, arising from beneath their mosquito bars, running along the shoreline while trying to put their clothes on and stay ahead of the skeeters. It was as bad or worse at Flamingo.

Tebeau's *Man in the Everglades* tells of a naturalist visiting Flamingo in 1893, finding it infested with fleas and mosquitoes. He declared he saw an oil lamp extinguished by a cloud of mosquitoes and noted each cabin at Flamingo was thickly sooted by constant use of smudge pots.

Shark River country does not mean isolation if you don't desire it. A marked back route goes to Flamingo from Little Shark River via Coot Bay. You'll see enough floating beer cans on weekends to signal you are not alone. A fixed bridge with a vertical clearance of 10 feet makes the back route to the Flamingo marina viable only for small craft and houseboats.

On the Gulf side there are three capes, all part of Cape Sable below the Little Shark River entrance. Their sandy beaches distinctly outline the shoreline and are useful in keeping track of the capes which are, from north to south, Northwest, Middle and East capes. The beach runs almost the entire length from East Cape to Middle Cape. Lake Ingraham lies protected behind the beach. Captain Frank Papy, who charters Florida Keys trips out of Miami, has Cape Sable on his itinerary.

(In his *Cruising Guide to the Florida Keys*, Frank reports the shelling there is terrific, with rarely anyone seen on the beach. When the water level is up, he says, it is possible to dinghy through the Middle Cape Canal into Lake Ingraham for some exploring and good fishing.)

The channel into Flamingo, nine miles from East Cape, varies in available water depths, but most shoal draft yachts can get in. It's a supply base, headquarters for park rangers, a haven to rest up after a bumpy ride across Florida Bay, as well as the place to arrange trips for bird watching.

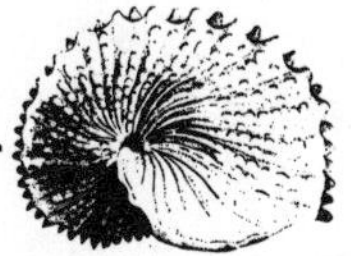

SMITTEN ON THE KEYS

Chapter 12

The Florida Keys lie between two altogether dissimilar places—downtown Miami and the Dry Tortugas islands out in the Gulf of Mexico. They begin at Virginia Key and extend in a crescent-shaped sweep to Loggerhead Key, a distance of about 192 miles. Loggerhead, some 65 miles west of Key West, is one in an 11-mile string of islands known collectively as the Dry Tortugas.

The Keys really don't stand alone for they have a shadow companion known as the Florida Reefs, a chain of reefs and shoals that lie an average of five miles out from the line of keys on the Atlantic Ocean side.

Motorists, inclined to reshape geography to the confines of a road map, are more likely to visualize the Keys as the 102 road miles between Key Largo and Key West.

The scientist, on the other hand, sees the upper keys as the bony skeleton of an ancient reef, the lower keys formed of egg-shaped limestone particles cemented together in a form of rock called Miami oolite.

There are different ways to explore the beauty of the Keys. One way, perhaps the best and most leisurely, is by boat. Others contend the real beauty is seen only by divers and snorkelers. A smaller, but persistent, group maintains the ideal perspective is gained by viewing the islands from a small airplane. The colors and patterns of the Keys are spread for miles along a narrow band stitched together by causeways and bridges.

Ideally, the Keys should be viewed from all perspectives—under, on and above the water. With a little planning, that could be done in a single vacation cruise.

It has been said that one either likes the Florida Keys or doesn't. The big comparative, of course, is the Bahamas with all their cruising beauties. But there are those who do not like the remoteness of some parts of the Bahamas, or are just more comfortable in staying "stateside."

As for clarity of the competitive waters, it's gin-clear in the Bahamas, vodka-clear in the Florida Keys. The transient tippler sails to both places, happy in either.

To some extent, the Keys get second billing to the Bahamas because many have the impression the waters are too shallow, especially for sailboats. But, if three to four feet is considered an ideal draft limit for the Bahamas close-to-shore anchoring, the same can be said of the Keys.

Captain Frank M. Papy, author of *Cruising Guide to the Florida Keys*, has been chartering trips between Miami, Key West and the Dry Tortugas for years. His booklet goes a long way toward dispelling

rumors there are few decent anchorages, charting as it does deeper water routes and many places to put the hook down.

It may be helpful to picture the keys in four sections: all of Biscayne Bay and the Biscayne National Monument area, Key Largo to Marathon, Marathon to Key West and Key West to Dry Tortugas.

Only the cruising skipper with unlimited time would make it a roundtrip. Some, with tight vacation schedules, cruise Miami to Marathon in leisurely fashion one year, from Marathon via Key West to Dry Tortugas the next. This requires getting the boat down to Marathon, more or less in sprint fashion on a long weekend, or moving it along in short stages.

What would a cruising skipper be doing if he were not planning another trip?

There are three routes to the Florida Keys. Two actually run alongside each other, separated by the chain of Florida Keys—Hawk Channel on the Atlantic side, the Intracoastal Waterway running through bays and sounds on the other. The third approach from the U.S. mainland is down the west coast of Florida, with a wide choice of departure points from Tarpon Springs on down to Naples. The latter port is often left by sailboats heading straight to the Dry Tortugas.

Cruising the Florida Keys can be far more enjoyable if you have some advance idea of the advantages and disadvantages of the routes.

Hawk Channel Route

This is often called the "outside run," favored by large powered craft, particularly by those involved in sports fishing, by those in a hurry and by deep draft (five feet or over) sailboats.

Hawk Channel, connecting Miami and Key West, is 127 nautical miles long and skirts the chain of keys, but remains inside the Florida Reefs in depths of water from nine to 34 feet. The average width is five miles, but at one point it narrows to about one-quarter of a mile.

Wind direction and its force play a role for skippers whose boats can go the "inside" route on Florida Bay as well as running Hawk Channel. In moderate to strong winds from west through north, Hawk affords more protection than Florida Bay. However, winter nor'westers that veer to the northeast can make Hawk Channel unpleasant.

In heavy, easterly weather, it is better to be on the bay side of the Florida Keys, if draft permits. Veering winds to the south and southeast tend to reduce the seas. In summer, weather is generally so routinely favorable that either route is free of wind direction problems.

While nine feet of water in Hawk is appealing to cruising skippers, it is important to remember there is long-range commitment involved. It's 80 statute miles from Cape Florida on Key Biscayne to the Channel 5 crossover from ocean to bay, 90 to Moser Channel at Marathon. The Marathon-Key West distance is 40 statute miles.

If the choice of whether to use Hawk Channel or the Intracoastal on the north side of the Keys seems weighty, at least there is the choice. Cruising the Maine coast, it's stay or go; in the Florida Keys, it's which way?

Hawk Channel presents a real need for experienced piloting and navigation. Any passage inside reefs, especially one that is well over 100 miles in length, automatically demands close attention. In many areas, lighted navigational aids and day markers are far apart, requiring that a compass course be steered.

Using the channel at night is risky. It is difficult to think of a reason why it should be used after dark by recreational craft, certainly not by anyone who considers himself on a pleasure-seeking cruise. Plan day trips along Hawk Channel. There are enough marinas, if the cruising schedule is properly planned, to make mid-afternoon stops. It is far better to pull in a little bit earlier than to have darkness come before some distant objective is reached.

One major advantage of using Hawk is that it is free of the influence of the northward-flowing Gulf Stream. The *Coast Pilot* indicates the current in Hawk Channel sets fair with the channel, except alongside the open area between Hawk and northern Biscayne Bay where a fairly strong cross-current exists, particularly on an ebb tide.

Guard against cross currents, especially near openings between the keys. Not only do strong currents exist on occasion, but there is also a pickup in wind strength as it blows through the land openings.

On a 1979 cruise, we went through Angelfish Creek at the north end of Key Largo to start working down the Keys, having already cruised the 30 miles of Biscayne Bay to Miami on several other occasions. We made it a point to pass through the creek on a slack current period. (Some do not go through either side of low tide.)

As we cruised *Final Edition* along the John Pennekamp State

Park, which stretches out for 21 miles, I recalled that I had read about a 60-passenger dive boat that had carried over 18,000 passengers to the park in 1976. It was ample evidence of the public fascination with underwater beauty in just one area.

Heading for Channel 5 at Lower Matecumbe Key, we approached Alligator Reef Light, which rises 136 feet above the reef. The underwater colors were so enticing we changed course and went out for a close-up look. No one could resist the temptation to get out the camera and start taking pictures. The Reef Light structure, octagonal with pyramidal skeleton framework, towered over snow-white, green and dark-blue patterns in the water, presenting a kind of marine mosaic.

In the Keys and the Bahamas, the apparent color of the water changes from day to day, even from hour to hour. The range of hues goes through greens, blues, pale yellow and purple. The sand reflects yellow rays in the shallows, green in deeper water. The water is, of course, colorless but it is the light, reflected upward from the bottom, that the eye sees. In the color code of the Keys, deeper blue means deeper water; rock and coral reflect blue while grass flats may appear deep purple or almost black under some conditions.

Our crossing over from Hawk Channel to the bay side at Channel 5 was routine because wind and current were favorable. We had noted earlier the 50 feet of *horizontal* clearance at the drawbridge, which, while enough on that day, might be difficult under the wrong wind and current conditions. An underpowered sailboat could have trouble.

We stayed well back in the channel after signalling the drawtender and noting his response. Most of the Keys drawtenders, we have found, are alert but often have to work with slow, antiquated equipment. If the approach is made too soon, and the draw doesn't open as quickly as you had estimated, it's like painting yourself into a corner.

Fortunately, plans call for some of the old bridges and equipment to be replaced in the coming years. One of the first scheduled for rebuilding is Seven Mile Bridge at Marathon, which means the Moser Channel draw will be replaced by modern machinery.

Hawk Channel off Marathon is used extensively by yachts going to or returning from Key West. Out of Marathon, there is the alternate choice of using Big Spanish Channel, often the choice of the more leisure-minded cruising people bound for Key West.

If Hawk Channel is faulted by some for not having many good anchorages between Angelfish Creek and Marathon, that's partially offset by Newfound Harbor, 20 miles west of Marathon. Jim Guy, writing in *Southern Boating*, terms it "perhaps the most popular cruising target in the middle Keys." There is adequate depth going in to Newfound, but it is advisable to have the depth indicator working to give the entrance buoy good clearance. The channel passes north of the Newfound Harbor Keys.

Anchorages are west of Big Pine Key and south of Little Torch Key. Deeper-draft yachts anchor nearer the channel entrance, but those drawing five feet or less proceed to the harbor. Mangrove islands surround the roughly circular harbor. It looked enough like a South Seas lagoon to be a site for the filming of the picture *PT Boat 109*. It is a protected area, ideal for fishing and swimming. Nearby, in Niles Channel, is an anchorage also used by cruising yachts. Five feet can be carried in. The anchorage is somewhat exposed to northerly winds, but the wave action is said not to be uncomfortable. Both areas, Niles and Newfound, are ideal for dinghy exploring, but their most valuable asset is that they provide a safe retreat from bad weather that might develop in Hawk Channel.

A Monumental Cruise

It is difficult for many people to realize they are cruising the Florida Keys when they still can see the skylines of Miami and Miami Beach. Some consider themselves to be in the Florida Keys only when the Florida mainland, let alone Miami, is no longer visible.

Biscayne Bay may be underrated in the overall Florida cruising scene despite its many fine cruisable features. Those who live close by and cruise it routinely many times a year may take it for granted. Others, who have never seen it, may merely assume that under the lee of such a huge metropolitan area as Miami, a major cruising ground could not survive with any measure of beauty retained.

The truth is that Biscayne Bay is easily one of Florida's finest cruising grounds. Those in Dade County who sought to preserve the bay, the islands, reefs, creeks and sounds, were the foot soldiers who made a metropolitan marine miracle possible.

The long, thin line of green islands separating Miami's South Biscayne Bay from the Atlantic are the north end of the Florida Keys. Most of the islands for some years have been in the protective fold of the Biscayne Bay National Monument under the control of the Department of the Interior. The Monument is made up of approxi-

mately 96,000 acres, 4,000 of which is land, including about 30 keys; the remainder includes offshore reefs and sandy bay bottom.

In the early 1960s, a bitter political battle raged over establishing the Monument. Opposing the conservationists were property owners on the islands, most of them on Elliott Key, 17 miles from Miami. The owners held 342 parcels of land covering over 4,300 acres and many of them favored developing the islands for waterfront hotels and high-rise apartments. Finally, in 1966, the Biscayne Bay National Monument was established, probably not a minute too soon.

The waters within the Monument confine are rich and varied in tropical life. Because the park borders the temperate and tropic zones, it has communities of plants of both zones on the land and in the waters.

The park's reefs are predominantly coral, both living and dead.

Woody vegetation covers the keys almost completely. Mangroves crowd the shoreline and on higher elevations a variety of tropical hardwoods, in the second growth period, can be found. In the 1800s, mahogany trees flourished on Elliott Key, but were eventually wiped out by lumbering operations. Madeira mahogany trees were carried off in schooners and reportedly sold for one dollar each.

Largest of the keys in the Biscayne National Monument is eight-mile-long Elliott Key, where there is a marina for boats that draw three-and-one-half feet or less. A 90-acre park provides good recreational facilities for cruisers who wish to go ashore. A path across the island leads to the oceanside picnic and barbecue area. The key is generally crowded on weekends, but with a choice of anchorages, the cruising fleet thins out. Sands Key, immediately north of Elliott, has several anchorages in bights along the west shoreline. The north half of Elliott also is popular.

Sands, Elliott and some of the other keys are great for anchoring when winds are easterly, but it's a different story in the winter if strong west winds sweep across the bay preceding a cold front. That could mean anchoring against a lee shore, which is contrary to cruising common sense.

Caesar Creek is popular, particularly with anglers, because it is a bay-to-Hawk Channel route, but it is something first-time cruising visitors should study. Captain Papy, in his guide, commends an anchorage right off the creek, south of Adams Key. It is necessary to get through a four-foot area, but once past, there are deep holes right off Adams Key, though current can run fairly strong. Park service buoys are helpful in guiding the uncertain.

Caesar Creek is named after the pirate, Black Caesar, a black who escaped from a slave ship. It is generally agreed that he started out as a singlehanded ship wrecker, probably working out of Elliott Key. The tactic of luring unwary sailors over the shoals brought him his first vessel.

Robert Roscoe, in *A Cruising Guide to the Southern Coast*, reports that for many years there was an iron ring embedded in a rock in Caesar Creek, a tiny island that bears his name. The story goes that Caesar used it to heel his ship so it could not be seen by passing vessels.

Black Caesar apparently traveled in the upper echelon of pirates, associating with Jean Lafitte and Blackbeard. It was Black Caesar's misfortune, however, to be aboard *Queen Ann's Revenge* when it was captured. After Blackbeard was killed in the fighting, Black Caesar tried to blow up the ship by dropping a match in a gunpowder magazine. The attempt failed and he was taken to Virginia and hanged.

Legend has it that Blackbeard left behind on Elliott Key a rather imposing harem of captured women, prisoners and children. Most of them eventually perished, but some of the children survived, speaking a language of their own creation. Seminole Indians, coming over from the mainland, heard the strange voices and concluded evil spirits haunted the islands. They avoided the area for years.

Two other creeks lie below Caesar, both just outside the southern boundary of the Monument. They are Broad Creek, difficult for a cruising boat to enter, and the much used Angelfish.

The Florida Keys Intracoastal

The Intracoastal Waterway, or "inside" route, that runs from Miami to Key West is a completely different kind of ICW than exists in the Norfolk-Miami version. There is no relatively deep water ditch to contain the larger cruising boats, and compass courses have to be steered through many miles of "skinny" water. If your boat draws more than five fieet—four is a more practical limit—settle for Hawk Channel. Otherwise, sample the delights of cruising the sounds and bays of the ICW.

It's a straightforward run down Biscayne Bay to Featherbed Bank, on a true course of about 193 degrees with plenty of water—much

more than will be found once Florida Bay is reached. Featherbed is 14 miles south of Miami; threading through shoals there and Cutter Bank beyond will be good practice for what is to come later. The well-marked channel leads through Card and Barnes sounds and presents no problems.

It is when passing through Jewfish Creek, 30 miles south of Miami, that many get the impression the "real" Florida Keys start. From there on, the cruising skipper will be dealing with Florida Bay for many miles to come. Florida Bay is described in the *Coast Pilot* as triangular-shaped, extending in a general east-west direction from Barnes Sound to Cape Sable. In the eastern part, depths are shallow and irregular, the bottom mostly coral with a thin covering of silt. The western sector is comparatively clear with depths of seven to 13 feet, covered with loggerhead sponges and small coral heads.

The ICW makes its way along a channel that is marked, but not regularly maintained through dredging. (It appears to us the only dredging done is supplied by the fanning action of hundreds of propellers that use the inside route.) Because of the shoals, careful navigation is necessary and early acceptance of that fact sets the pattern of watchfulness.

Current water depth information on the channel from Biscayne Bay through Florida Bay is difficult to obtain. An early 1980 study provides some general knowledge, though not indicative of what the depths might be at this reading.

The U.S. Corps of Engineers, in a report dated February 7, 1980, listed mid-channel depths at mean low water for four regions: for 36.8 miles from Miami southward, the controlling depth (lowest) was 4.7 feet. That does not mean it was that low everywhere, but it was so in at least one place. In the next eight miles, the shallowest area at average low tide was 5.9 feet. Two other least-depth recordings were 5.4 feet between ICW mile 1135 and Boggy Creek, and 4.4 feet near Plantation Key.

The project depth for the waterway is seven feet. "Project" depth is what the Corps of Engineers plan and strive for, but the controlling depth is what counts. One three-foot area can nullify miles of 10-foot water either side of it. Keep posted with *Local Notice to Mariners* for depth changes.

Boat traffic remains high on the Florida Bay waterway channel. Those who understand the draft limits make it through. The depth indicator should be kept on and the lookout should use Polaroid glasses to sort out color characteristics in the water ahead, watching especially for bars encroaching into the channel edges.

In the Keys, the problem of piloting through shallow water can be eased by avoiding eastward runs in the first morning hours and westward cruising in the late afternoon. Not only is it more difficult to see the channel edges, but the eye strain can be considerable.

Newcomers to the Florida Keys are often disturbed by a trail of clouded water in their wake. It is unlikely the boat is scraping bottom; what is seen is powdery sand stirred by the propeller.

The Intracoastal, going west, leads to Bahia Honda Key, beyond Marathon. At Marathon, the choice is whether to cross over to Hawk Channel or go on to Big Spanish Channel, leaving Florida Bay and entering Gulf waters.

One other marked channel in Florida Bay that should be studied for possible use is the Yacht Channel which meets the Intracoastal at a lighted black beacon on Old Dan Bank northwest of Layton. The channel crosses northwest from there to Cape Sable and meets the approach to a channel leading east to Flamingo. The route is marked with lighted navigational aids three to seven miles apart. The yacht channel is convenient if one wishes to depart Cape Sable and cross Florida Bay to Islamorada.

We have used it after leaving an anchorage at Shark River, skirting Cape Sable and going on to an anchorage at Shell Key, near Islamorada. We logged it at 46.5 nautical miles. For those entering the Florida Keys from the west coast for the first time, the yacht channel provides a practical indoctrination into piloting through typical shallow waters in the Keys.

The Florida Bay Scene

Florida Bay is a sprawling body of shallow water that can be walked in, if not on, freckled as it is with countless mangrove and sandbar islands. There are even "lakes" within the bay waters.

The boundaries of Everglades National Park embrace nearly all of Florida Bay. Park area markers are seen on the north side of the Intracoastal Waterway from Jewfish Creek to the yacht channel that cuts diagonally across the bay. Within the borders gather numerous bird watchers, naturalists, shallow-water fishermen and collectors of bottles and shells.

It is a part of the Keys probably not visited by most cruising people

because of the shallow water. But others make it a point to get there to view the vast concentration of birdlife that is especially abundant in the winter months.

In winter, the bald eagle is almost certain to be seen. There are several nests on islands as well as on the mainland, all carefully protected by the national park rangers.

The more experienced Florida Bay cruising skippers of medium-sized, shallow-draft boats know how to find their way into the small, but fairly deep, depressions in the bay bottom. They are sometimes referred to as lakes, useful as an anchorage and as a base to work out of with a small boat.

Most helpful to those interested in that area is a small, illustrated book written by John O'Reilly called *Boater's Guide to the Upper Florida Keys.* It concentrates on the area from Jewfish Creek to Long Key, and describes many interesting places that can be reached only by dinghies or by outboard and stern-drive-powered craft. Several charts show small boat routes.

O'Reilly writes: "The bay has many moods. Sometimes in the heat of summer there will be periods of virtually no wind when the water surface stretches away like an endless mirror. Faraway places take on odd shapes. Distant boats seem to be floating in air because the horizon is indistinguishable. When the winter winds blow strong, the bay becomes a mass of choppy, whitecapped waves. At these times the water will become milky white as the marl of the bottom is stirred by wave action.

"At other times the water will be crystal clear. Water colors in the bay are always changing because of the light conditions, shifting clouds and the amount of the marl stirred up. In the summer the towering cumulus clouds build up to bring squalls and thunder showers, but as night falls they also bring those gaudy sunsets for which Florida Bay is famous. All these aspects of nature combine to make those who know the bay love it."

Parts of Florida Bay provide excellent fishing. O'Reilly makes the observation that some Keys natives will eat only fish that come from Florida Bay, a finny fidelity unsurpassed in fish-rich Florida.

For most who go to the Florida Keys, the "action" is on the south side of the Intracoastal. The 60 miles between Key Largo and Marathon are the available-people zone, with several marinas, restaurants, fishing tackle and bait emporiums and sundry other facilities ready to cater to the desires of the cruising-vacationing fraternity.

A non-commercial stopover which is becoming increasingly popular is Lignumvitae Key, now operated as a Florida state park. It is the only place in the Keys where tropical hardwoods grow naturally in a virgin forest. The key, a short distance west of Islamorada, has an elevation of 16 and one-half feet, notable only in that it is the highest of all the keys.

You don't have to be a botanist to appreciate lignum vitae and ironwood trees in their natural state. Both woods were once popularly used in the building of ships. Lignum vitae is so hard that for many years it was used to make propeller shaft bearings, while ironwood was manufactured into trunnels (tree nails) to fasten heavy timber together.

The cliché that "when you see one island in the Florida Keys, you've seen them all," overlooks that some have interesting backgrounds and have played a role in history. Lignumvitae Key has attracted the attention of men for years, dating back to the known occupation of it by Calusa Indians, who created a burial mound there. Spaniards lumbered it, but also built a coral rock wall—3,000 feet long—in which to contain slaves.

In 1919, the island was purchased by W. J. Matheson of Miami. Matheson imported trees, Mexican burros, turtles from the Galápagos, angora goats from India and rabbits from Guyana, turning them loose on the heavily forested island.

Today, the island, as a state park, has a less exotic animal population. There is limited dockage for small craft. Cruising boats anchor out from the dock, with crews going ashore in dinghies. Two-hour walking tours are provided.

Indian Key is located near Lignumvitae Key, but on the Atlantic side of what is U. S. Highway 1. Sometime prior to 1700, some 400 Frenchmen were said to have been massacred there by Indians. The Spanish, arriving later and hearing about the massacre, called it Matanzas, or Slaughter Island.

Marathon: Keys Pivot Point

For many, Marathon is the west end of the Florida Keys, particularly for those interested in fishing. The nearest rival of consequence is Islamorada, which has a large, loyal following of light-tackle anglers who seem to concentrate on bonefish, permit and tarpon on the

flats and channels of Florida Bay.

Marathon, however, is so positioned that its fishing fleet can work the Gulf Stream or the nearby Seven Mile and Bahia Honda bridges as well as the bonefish flats.

Geographically, Marathon is a pivot point, a turnaround for a return to Miami, a gathering place for west coast yachts coming to the Keys, or a starting point for cruises in different directions as well as a community with an extensive array of marine services. If you have to experience a breakdown in the Keys, Marathon is a handy place for it.

There are marinas on both sides of Marathon. Depending on what one calls a harbor, the Florida Keys have only two or three. One is Marathon's Boot Key Harbor which has two marked channels leading into it from Hawk Channel. There is also room to anchor in a protected area.

Boot Key Marina is a famous name among Intracoastal Waterway travelers and is a rendezvous for cruising types, many of whom assemble there for the winter. There is a large sailboat colony within the marina but powerboats are also welcomed.

One of the most talked-about features is the sundown gathering of members of the Boot Key Marina community on a "bring your own" basis. As a result, it can be said that many friendships have been fashioned over some old-fashioneds as the sunset was toasted down for the day.

Our first cruise into Marathon was in 1954 and in subsequent trips we made many friends and acquaintances along the waterfront. Thus, it was particularly painful to see Marathon after Hurricane Donna got through with it in 1960. It was thought then Marathon would be doomed in terms of population growth, but such was not to be the case. Now, there are too many people, and seemingly every fifth office houses a real estate agent.

Still, the local laundromat manages to retain some of the old-time humor. Last time Peggy and I visited it, the big dryers had pasted on them such names as Good Old Betsy, Hard Working Sally and Our Best Girl. Peggy settled for one named Red Hot Annie.

At Faro Blanco Marina, which old-timers remember as the Davis docks, we look forward to a reunion with a great white heron known as Willoughby, of whom we have written considerably over the years. Willoughby is a classic freeloader. Natural fishing grounds for herons like Willoughby are within sight of the marina, but that would be too much work, a show of honest labor.

Willoughby is strictly on the bum, not only panhandling along the dock, but given to stealing bits of shrimp or cut bait out of the buckets of unsuspecting tourists fishing from the docks and catwalks. He is always around when the boats come in from a day of fishing and there are fish to clean. That's when Willoughby, long of leg, white as a freshly laundered bedsheet, moves in. His initial tactic is to adopt the positive stance, elevate his long neck to the fullest and give you that steady, never-blink stare which can go on and on until you think that his eyes are artificial and of glass, somehow pinned on. He stands motionless and you feel you are looking at an Aubdubon color plate.

Willoughby seems to be out of reaching range for any falling tidbit of fish from the cleaning stand, but he has figured the distance precisely. His feet can be in one place but his neck and bayonet beak can shoot out a yardstick's length farther, a split-second extension that is always right on target.

The velocity comes out of a neck recoil, springlike action. He gets the fish scrap with such refined accuracy that I am convinced Willoughby could pick a wallet and take a $5 bill out from between two $10s without rustling the currency.

Well, alongside *Final Edition* one day at Faro Blanco, a man came in with more fish than he really needed. As he cleaned away, Peggy admonished me for not going out ourselves and catching a supply of fish, the more so since both of us are seafood lovers. A short time later, the fisherman approached our boat with a handful of fillets, asking if we would like them.

I enthusiastically accepted, thanked him and paid sincere tribute to his angling skill. Peggy smiled but gave me one of those family looks that sends a clear unspoken message. She wouldn't say it, but she was telling me I was just another Willoughby myself, too lazy to catch my own fish but willing to accept the first fresh fillet offered.

It occurred to me that I really do have the habit while cruising of getting as near as possible to the fish cleaning stand when tying up *Final Edition.* At Yankeetown, I saw a man cleaning cobia and sure enough he offered us a beautiful, big fillet.

Later, he came by our boat and asked if we minded eating shark. He had been cleaning cobia, to be sure, but he had caught, dressed out and iced down a small sand shark earlier in the day.

"The trick is to clean 'em right away, get the fillets on ice," he said. "I catch quite a few of them. They eat right good."

And, by golly, it did.

Big Spanish to Key West

From Marathon, the anchor-out, island-hopping cruising buff headed for Key West is liable to spend two or three days, perhaps more, covering the 52 miles between the best known cities in the Keys. We last cruised it in 1979 and stretched it out to three days.

Most call it the Big Spanish Channel route, which starts north of the Bahia Honda bridges and travels northwest into Gulf waters.

Willoughby, a great white heron and regarded as a white morph of the great blue heron, is one of the sights at Faro Blanco Marina at Marathon in the Keys. Note the crest on his head and the way he peers into the water around the rocks, ready to capture small, bait-size fish. The pelican making a pile-inspection stopover is common in the area.
Marston photo

Some make much of piloting through Big Spanish Channel, which twists and turns its way through day markers at the northern end, but it is no great exercise in decent weather. It would be something else again in a nor'wester, but few cruisers take on the Gulf when that condition prevails.

Once into the Gulf, it is a matter of moving southwestward along the keys in deep water with a course shaped to Smith Shoal Light, about two miles north of the bell buoy designating the entrance to

Key West's Northwest Channel.

Twenty-three nautical miles out of Marathon we turned off Big Spanish Channel just north of No Name Key. A couple of hundred yards farther on we found a 10-foot spot west of Porpoise Key. There was plenty of room and only one sailboat to share it with.

The top third of Big Pine Key was to the west of us. It is a big, sprawling key where the best known residents are the federally protected key deer in the refuge at the north end of the island and on Howe Key. When full-grown, the deer are between 20 and 32 inches high at the shoulder and weigh between 30 and 110 pounds; the averages are 65 for the buck, 40 for the doe.

Our passage through the northwestern end of Big Spanish Channel was on a beautiful, windless day. The channel edges could be easily seen. In coming out of Big Spanish into the Gulf, once past Harbor Key Bank Light it was clear going in 18 feet of water. But we had not gone far along when we decided to go in Cudjoe Channel, keeping Riding Key to starboard. It was not a planned thing, just something that looked attractive on the chart and worth investigating. The deep water off Tarpon Belly Key made it a natural place for anchoring.

Study the chart before entering Cudjoe Channel, making sure the entrance course clears the four-foot shoal on Crane Key. We headed for Riding Key and kept it fairly close to starboard. There was up to 10 feet of channel water to work with, leading to a good anchorage right off Tarpon Belly Key. If you like strange anchorage names in the log, Tarpon Belly is hard to beat.

Just beyond the anchorage, numerous markers on the inside route from No Name Key to Key West can be seen. The route, much too shallow for cruising boats and not maintained, nevertheless looks like an interesting dinghy trip. Two veteran cruising friends of ours, Bruce and Wanda Bidwell, actually made it in a small sailboat but had to drag it over one two-foot spot. The markers, while numbered, do not show ICW markings; they guide one through a winding route still used in parts by local fishermen.

What really dominated our anchorage was a large moored blimp on a key about two miles from us. We could see all but the gondola. Windows were painted over and the entire body was white, as though it had been given a coat of whitewash with a fire hose. We broke out the dinghy and got close enough to see that it was within an area surrounded by a chainlink fence. There were evidences of tight security.

We later found that what we were looking at was locally nicknamed Fat Albert, a remarkable surveillance vehicle that could be sent up tethered by a very long cable. A part of the U.S. defense system, it had the capability of even seeing the traffic lights in Havana but, more importantly, also looked down on military movements, including a Russian garrison.

Our weird-looking, ghostly pale, very important anchorage neighbor met an untimely end in early 1980. A tornado demolished the blimp while it was secured at its base on Cudjoe Key. Fat Albert was thereafter sorely missed by many, including us, who had become used to his plump presence in the lee of Tarpon Belly Key.

But years before Fat Albert arrived, the Cudjoe area had had another strange local feature. On nearby Sugarloaf Key, an Englishman named C. W. Chase started a sponge farm in 1910. It was a good idea but thieves kept stealing the product of his enterprise to the point Chase sold the business and a large tract of land to Richter C. Perkey during World War I.

According to the informative little publication, *The Key Guide*, by George B. Stevenson of Tavernier, Perkey was not interested in sponges but did develop the area as a resort. He built a large restaurant, a gambling casino, cottages and, interestingly enough, two bat towers.

The towers were to house imported bats that would clear the area of mosquitoes. But the bats, badly outnumbered and outgunned, soon disappeared. The mosquitoes then turned their attention to the human high rollers down at the casino. No gambler who had lost his shirt betting could survive the mosquitoes. The development failed. The bats were Mr. Perkey's last resort.

West of Tarpon Belly Key is Johnston Key Channel, which has two good anchoring locations, fine except in the northwest winds of winter. Although the anchorages are not far from Tarpon Belly, it is necessary to go back out Cudjoe and come in the channel to Johnston.

From Tarpon Belly Key, it was a half-day run to Key West. Rather than compete for limited space in Key West proper, we continued on through Northwest Channel to Hawk Channel, then went to the Key West Oceanside Marina after first checking by radio for space availability. Located on Stock Island, it is a large marina built in 1972. Its drawback is that it is a bus or taxi cab ride into Key West. Its advantage, to those wishing to go east to Marathon or beyond, is that it is just off Hawk Channel.

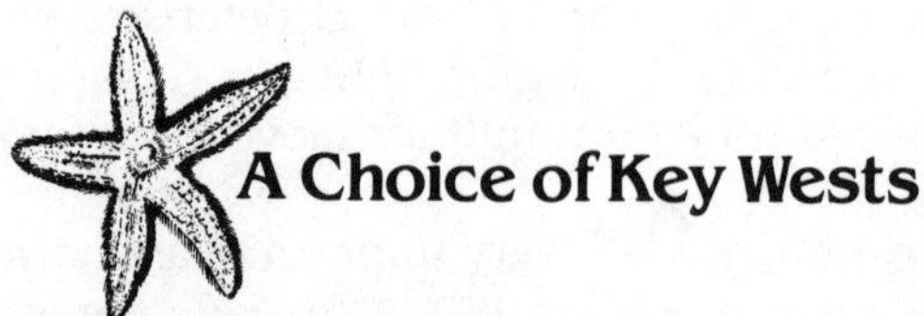

A Choice of Key Wests

The only publicity Key West needs is good publicity. It would seem that so much has been written about historic old Key West, its former literary colony and its modern-day problems that nothing much of value can be added.

Probably the biggest mistake that can be made is to see Key West for only a few hours and then shove off. Like many other noted places, it requires some understanding, and that takes more than a half-day of assessment.

Like New York City, Key West is a seek-and-ye-shall find-it place. Few cities have suffered as much as it has from repeated highs and lows in economy, hurricanes, or being a military city with all the advantages and disadvantages that go with that. The Old Island, as old-timers often think of it, has a heritage that goes back to the Indians, the Spanish Conquistadors and the Caribbean pirates.

An international seaport, it has been more than a mere port of call to thousands of seafaring people, some who brought their architectural culture and culinary skills ashore with them. The Cubans came early and late; in 1980 over 100,000 fled Cuba, the majority of them first putting into Key West in a sea lift that reminded some of Dunkirk. Bahamians arrived many decades ago as did the straight-laced New Englanders, those wily merchants who mingled with the southern aristocrats.

Key West was linked to the mainland in 1912 when Henry M. Flagler completed his grand dream, the Overseas Railroad, which ran 122 miles from Homestead. Then the highway came, but during its construction hundreds were killed in hurricanes and storms. There was always a price to pay to get to Key West and a price to pay to stay, but that's true of most worthy objectives. Key West is still an island seaport town. The shrimpers, with a fleet numbering more than 400, work and play hard.

Tourists come by the thousands, including all of us who come by boat. Key West merchandises history but so do Newport, Charleston, Boston, San Francisco and New Orleans, among others. Key West sometimes has visitors that some would rather not have, footloose transients who summer at Provincetown on Cape Cod and come in

Key West's waterfront is one of the most publicized in the nation. Key West is the country's southernmost city, probably the only truly tropical city in the continental U.S. Slip space in the city proper is limited. One of the best known waterfront establishments is the Pier House, shown here. It provides customer accommodations. Marston photo

the winter to the city at the end of the line, pieces of human driftwood scattered along the high-tide mark. They themselves become a sort of tourist attraction.

Peggy and I thoroughly enjoyed a visit to the Audubon House. But, then, I also liked my first visit to Sloppy Joe's bar several years ago. Key West has that kind of range. It's another good walking town. There are good restaurants and seedy ones, the usual highs and lows.

In Key West, try a Spanish restaurant and order the works: Cuban bread, picadillo, black beans and rice and flan. For breakfast, it was recommended that we get up early and go down to the Fisherman's Café on Caroline Street, where one cup of Cuban coffee should be enough to wake up anyone.

Walk down to the harbor or rent a bicycle. Pedal around the island or just stroll along, listen to the sounds, smell the odors from kitchens, observe the lush vegetation, and try to capture the feel for the city that attracted Ernest Hemingway, Tennessee Williams, President Harry Truman and John James Audubon.

As writer Frank Sargeant observed in *Sea* magazine, "Key West

looks, feels and smells like a foreign country, but the only passport required is a sound hull and a ready crew."

You can walk the width of the downtown Key West area, from the Gulf to the Atlantic, in about 20 minutes. Remember you are walking in the footsteps of ship wreckers, pirates, crewmen from Spanish galleons, sailors from Boston and Salem.

Near sunset, be at Mallory Dock and don't be astounded if the audience boos or claps at the quality of the sunset. The town's own established "characters" will be there, along with would-be eccentrics, drifters, Ivy Leaguers, startled tourists, babies, assorted animals and the usual assortment of guitar pluckers. You'll see wine being sipped and on a calm night the smell of pot might well hang over groups of people. That's not all Key West, just a part of it.

The lucky ones are those who cruise in, leisurely savor the old island, and can look forward to tomorrow's cruise out to the Dry Tortugas.

Dry Tortugas: Fortress in the Sea

There is one place within the cruising world of Florida that is set apart from all others. It's out there in the Gulf of Mexico, 63 nautical miles west of Key West. Though attainable, it is just far enough and remote enough to keep from being overrun by a steady stream of boats.

It is true that with the high-speed runabouts of today and customized console-type sportsfishermen in the 26-foot size, some can make the 130-mile round trip, in a weekend of good weather, for fishing or diving. Fuel considerations have cut back on that traffic to some extent but it still is done by many who find that a sleeping bag and a large cooler of iced-whatevers provide the essentials for a short stay.

To most, however, a cruise out to the Dry Tortugas can be the highlight of a summer cruise, something looked forward to for months, something carefully planned. There are people who own boats almost for the sole purpose of faithfully going to the Dry Tortugas every year.

Anyone planning a first trip to the Dry Tortugas must understand

A favorite Florida offshore stop for cruisers is Fort Jefferson, on Garden Key in the Dry Tortugas. The lighthouse on the fort is part of a half-mile-long brick enclosure of sixteen acres. The development of the rifled cannon made the fort obsolete early in its history. Converted to a prison, its most famous prisoner was Dr. Samuel A. Mudd, the physician who set the broken leg of John Wilkes Booth.
Marston photo

there is no fuel, water, food, ice, electricity or marina space there. You must bring along whatever it takes to get there, stay there and get back.

There are seven islands in the group. To most, one island—Garden Key—is the Dry Tortugas. It is on Garden that Fort Jefferson is located, dating back to 1846 when it was planned as the largest fort in a comprehensive coastal defense system. It was designed for 450 guns and an operating force of 1,500 men.

As a fort, it saw no action. The development of the rifled cannon

made all masonry forts obsolete by the time of the Civil War. Fort Jefferson, however, turned to another career which was to make it an historic landmark. During the Civil War, Key West was the only city in Florida that remained under Union control. The fort became a prison for Confederate soldiers.

The most famous inmate was Dr. Samuel Mudd, the doctor who set John Wilkes Booth's broken leg after the assassination of President Lincoln. During a yellow fever epidemic in 1867, Dr. Mudd worked heroically to save the lives of the prisoners and guards. Dr. Mudd received a pardon, but it took many years to go beyond the pardon and gain complete exoneration.

The fort, now a national monument, is still an incredible sight, rising up in the open Gulf of Mexico as if it were an American Devil's Island. Built of brick, the fort is a half-mile around enclosing 16 acres, with parapets towering 50 feet above the waters of the moat that surrounds it.

The cruise from Key West is not difficult in good weather, but it shouldn't be attempted in anything but favorable conditions. An able boat and an experienced boat operator are necessary for the cruise out and back. The waters between Key West and the Dry Tortugas can be very rough and currents can run strong. Under those circumstances, it is no place for the novice.

More than any other place in the Keys, weather forecasts must be faithfully monitored in the Dry Tortugas. When you are in the island group, there is no short run for cover—only a long run for it. Thus, cruises sometimes have to be cut short by leaving with the first early warning, or remaining in the reasonably protected Garden Key area. The keys help break the seas in a storm. Fishing boats seek the protected waters of the keys in stormy periods, a clue that pleasure boat skippers should take into account when trying to decide whether to leave or stay.

Dry Tortugas:

There are two routes to the Tortugas from Key West. One runs south of the Marquesas Keys, about 20 miles from Key West; the other goes north of those keys. Departures from Key West are either through Southwest or Northwest channels. A common reference for yachts going either route is the Rebecca Shoal Light, 43 miles west of Key West.

Our choice was the north route. Conditions were right for it; not only right, but ideal, with just a light wind out of the south. After clearing Northwest Channel, our first leg took us 15.5 miles to Ellis Rock. Peggy's course called for a 10-degree change to a 262-degree heading to be held for 35.5 miles. The automatic pilot was put to work. An occasional slight change was made to correct for current drift.

Rebecca came up on course. As we drew nearer to Southeast Channel leading into Garden Key, we became aware that we were being pushed off the desired course. Using Loggerhead Key Light, a couple of miles beyond Garden Key, for a reference point, we were able to establish how much influence the tidal current was having on *Final Edition*.

Boats with radio direction finders can pick up a good signal from Loggerhead Key for corrections or affirmations of course. The return to Key West can also be navigationally assisted by tuning to the Key West station.

You may ask what there is for cruising people if there are no facilities at Fort Jefferson or on any of the other keys. There are several answers. The fishing is excellent. Diving and snorkeling are outstanding, in beautiful, clear waters. There are keys to visit (Loggerhead is one of the favorites). There is the satisfaction of being in a place where there is peace and quiet, room to move about in a unique offshore setting.

For the bird watchers, either dedicated or casually interested, Garden and Bush keys are meccas, particularly in the April to July nesting season. Hundreds of thousands of sooty and noddy terns come from all the Americas to Bush Key. Landing of boats on Bush is not permitted, but Garden Key is so close that there is a grandstand view. (The use of small boats, however, is permitted for observing afloat.) Garden Key itself is used by a vast number of different birds. Being without a bird book in the Dry Tortugas is like being in Aspen without skis in the winter.

Most cruising boats use the Garden Key anchorage as headquarters. Day trips or longer stays are made to some of the other keys. Others set up in a good location and use the dinghy for beach parties, fishing, diving and other recreational pursuits. Camping and cooking ashore are permitted, but only in designated areas.

Upon arrival at Garden, it is a good idea to check in with the park ranger office by briefly mooring at the 250-foot concrete and wooden pier. A copy of the rules and regulations will be made available. (An occasional gripe is heard about that, but it is a fact of life that

without some regulation vandals would literally make off with the fort, brick by brick. There was a period, before park personnel took up residence, when considerable damage was done. Modest restrictions are a small price to pay for being able to cruise to the Dry Tortugas and stay there for extended periods.)

The fort was abandoned in 1874, but was made a naval base during the Spanish-American War. The battleship *Maine* left Garden Key in early February, 1896, for Havana, where it was blown up, precipitating the United States' entry into the war. Fort Jefferson was a seaplane base in World War I, and an observation post in WWII. It has led a rather useful life considering it was declared obsolete not long after it was constructed.

There is an eerie air about it that not even hurricane winds blow away. When we are standing on the edge of the parade grounds, it all seems part of something Hollywood built. Yet, it is the real thing and it would not be surprising if Dr. Mudd appeared any minute.

The walk atop the walls of the fort provides a magnificent view of the surrounding waters, almost as high as the soaring birds. They fly by in profusion, one a blue-faced booby spotted by Peggy. To see one almost requires being on some island well out to sea, for it is their nature to nest on remote oceanic islands in the tropical seas.

To be at anchor off Garden Key, under the lee of the famous old fort, can be one of the great thrills of Florida cruising.

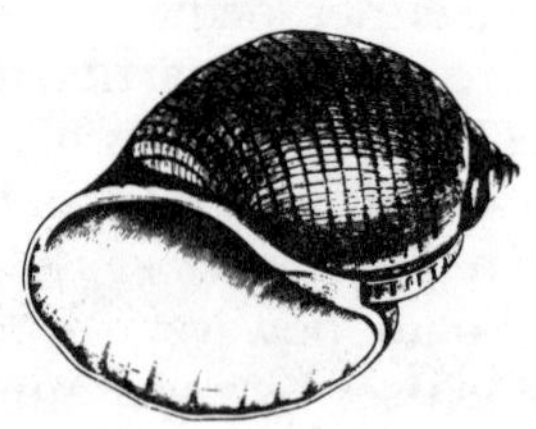

OKEECHOBEE RURAL ROUTE CRUISING

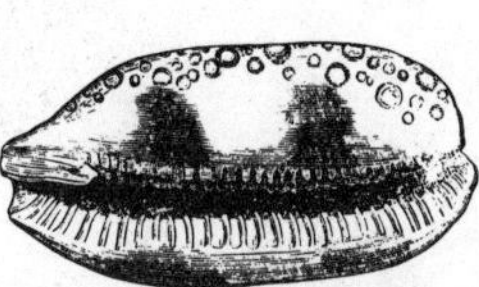

Chapter 13

There are only two reasons why you might not be able to cruise the Okeechobee waterway. There's a vertical limit of 49 feet, which excludes some sailboats, and a controlling draft depth of eight feet. Otherwise, there's no reason not to. There's probably a little country in most of us, anyway. No matter how much we love the sea—cruising along coast lines, circling islands, gunkholing, poking around rivers—to take a boat and go rural-route cruising can be a wonderful change of pace for the restless rovers of the waterways.

Most everyone is familiar with picture postcard Florida, but if you want to see the "un-Florida" Florida, cruise through it between the Atlantic Ocean and the Gulf of Mexico along the Okeechobee Waterway. Most of its 155 miles is through cattle and citrus country. In other spots it skirts lush vegetable farms and sugar cane fields that lie just beyond viewing range, hidden behind levees.

It's a chance to lock yourself up inside old Florida and look around for a few days. After all, not everyone gets to go yachting through someone's cattle ranch.

There is a certain intimacy that goes with the cross-state cruising. You cruise by old homes, or new ones made to look old, with big screened porches set back under the shade of giant oak trees. There are little towns along the way, each with a character and flavor of its own. Some hold swamp cabbage festivals, or a special day to honor the speckled perch and one, Indiantown, has its own little stadium for rodeos.

Cattle come down steep embankments to graze along the waterway, some of them wading knee-deep into the water to gain relief from the blazing sun of a summer afternoon. They do not flee the cruising boats, but rather turn their heads to make what appears to us a glum appraisal of the passing craft. They are the deadpan Buster Keatons of the bovine world.

Occasionally, a high-powered boat will come roaring along, throwing an udder-shaking wake that will drive them from the water. They don't like those curling walls of water, but neither do most humans.

I remember easing along in *Final Edition* one quiet winter morning. Somewhere, east of Lake Okeechobee between Indiantown and the St. Lucie lock, I got a sudden whiff of cow manure, not really offensive, but strangely unnautical and foreign to one who sails and cruises extensively. Then I began to hear cattle sounds, the old barnyard music. I thought, what am I doing up here on the flying bridge, sniffing *manure?*

It was alien to the world of my choice, which is liberally seasoned with salt while playful dolphins cruise at our heels like puppy dogs

The Okeechobee Waterway cuts across Florida between Fort Myers Beach on the Gulf of Mexico and Stuart on the Atlantic. It offers a 155-mile journey through cattle and citrus country. It provides rural route cruising, with cattle stoically positioned along the waterway, seemingly indifferent to passing sail and power boats.
Marston photo

begging for attention. But then, another year, what was I doing cruising down the Laguna Madre on the Texas Gulf Intracoastal being eyed suspiciously by coyotes who had crossed mudflats and come to the water's edge?

How do you convince people you have cruised among the coyotes of Texas, the Brahmas and Santa Gertrudis of the Florida cattle lands? Along with the smells and sounds, there are special sights for those who cruise the coast-to-coast incision below the belt line of the Florida peninsula.

It may be something as strikingly simple as the sight of a stately great blue heron surveying his domain, the wind ruffling his tail feathers and giving the impression his feathery frock is on the tattered side. A great loner except during the March mating season in Florida, he will stand for hours in shallow water waiting for something to come along.

Unless the fishing is good at the moment, he will fly away at the approach of a boat. It is an ungainly takeoff, as might be expected from a creature almost five feet tall. Overly long, thin legs have to be bent and positioned to spring back up with the flapping of wings that may spread out 70 inches overall. It is a labored liftoff, at best.

Then there are the interesting inanimate views, the octagonal-shaped house, for instance, that sits on a high bluff that is really a large mound of dirt thrown up by some long-ago dredging of the waterway. It's an unusual house, with picture windows, architecturally foreign to other homes in the cattle ranchlands, yet commanding and aloof up there on its barren perch. Curiosity is increased when you see the small airplane tied down near one corner of the house, a yellow school bus at the opposite end. It is an odd coupling of vehicles out in the boondocks.

Cruising and musing. Here and there, too, a touch of humor. Hundreds who cruised by must have seen a man sitting in a camp chair outside his tent atop an embankment waving cheerily as the boats went by. The campsite, a few miles east of Indiantown, was at the edge of a clearing behind which was an orange grove.

We looked for the man with mild, pleasant speculation. Then one day the chair was empty, though the tent was still up. Our searching eyes finally focused on a man sitting on a motorcycle. His right hand was raised aloft in greeting but, as we waved in return, something was wrong. The man never lowered his arm.

Peggy reached for her binoculars and soon laughed. On the propped-up motorcycle was a fully clothed dummy. We have wondered from time to time about that mute salute. Was the camper hidden from sight in the bushes, doubled over with laughter as we waved to the dummy? Or was he off on some mission not requiring the use of his motorcycle, but wanting everyone to know that his replacement was keeping faith with the passing strangers along the waterway?

Better a friendly wave from a dummy than none at all; such was the consensus aboard *Final Edition.*

There are places to pull off the waterway. Most of them make excellent one-or two-boat snug anchorages. There are a few a short

distance east of the Franklin Lock, above Fort Myers. They were created when the Caloosahatchee portion of the official waterway was straightened.

We have, on occasion, parted rafts of water hyacinth barring the opening to one of the almost-hidden retreats to let *Final Edition* find her way in at creeping speed. The hyacinth regroup behind us and we are all but sealed in; a tree and a bush-topped small island is the barrier between us and the Okeechobee Waterway. A rise of land crowned with moss-draped oaks is on our other side. You could cruise by without seeing us in there.

Peggy and I agree we'd rather be in some selected place along the Okeechobee Waterway in a hurricane than most any other place in Florida. There undoubtedly are good hurricane holes off the St. Johns River, up the Shark River and along the Gulf Intracoastal Waterway west of Apalachicola, but the Okeechobee has an extra advantage or two. Because of its lock system, there is no tidal surge to worry about. And it is the rapid buildup of tidal water in most hurricanes that causes more damage than the force of winds.

In one of the off-the-waterway little anchorages, where the natural course of the Caloosahatchee River once flowed, we'd take our chances with even a severe hurricane. The anchor scope would be short, but there would be the chance to tie-off to the lower branches of medium-sized tropical trees. Seas would not come pounding in. Surge would be minimal.

A thorough sounding of the area by dinghy for stumps or logs beneath the surface is advisable before establishing the best spot to anchor; give consideration also to trees that might fall. Otherwise, few places we know offer more storm security. There is only one drawback: a lot of other people know this, too.

Florida's Liquid Center

If you look at a map of Florida, that big hole about two-thirds of the way down the peninsula is Lake Okeechobee. It is slightly off-center, only 39 miles from the Atlantic coast and about 78 miles from the Gulf of Mexico. It is also 90 miles above the tip of the Florida mainland.

School children in Florida learn early that Lake Okeechobee is the second largest freshwater lake wholly within the confines of the Unites States. (Lake Michigan is the largest.) Boat owners who consider crossing it probably would like to know more about it.

The shape of the lake has been described as nearly circular, its width from 22 to 30 miles. It has about 750 square miles of open water, a shallow lake, only about 10 to 14 feet deep in the center and much less elsewhere. Probably 90 percent of the year its waters are docile, but then maybe that's what is also said of Albemarle Sound, the Delaware River and the long New Jersey coast line.

It's no place to be in a hard blow from the west to northwest. There are two routes of navigation, neither of them great, but one worse than the other in a winter nor'wester. That's the time to stay in port or remain at anchor working on the income tax or changing the oil filters.

Some 10,000 years ago, the lake was a hollow in the sea floor, but gradually filled up with vast deposits of sediment, erosion, and fantastic amounts of rain water that flowed into it from as far north as where Orlando is now.

In the late 1800s, an engineer named Isham Randolph described Okeechobee as "the great liquid heart of Florida." The lake has long sustained South Florida, irrigating the rich vegetable and sugar cane fields that rim its shores, storing drinking water for the West Palm Beach-Miami megalopolis and serving as a bit of paradise for the dedicated bass fishermen.

But it has been a battleground in the name of drainage and flood control for well over 100 years. The most recent claim is that the flood control authorities, with the backing of powerful agricultural interests, are not so much engaged in water control as they are in land reclamation at public expense. The Florida Wildlife Federation has charged that millionaires have been made overnight.

It would be nice to say that, ecologically, it is a pristine lake that has endured, and by some miracle has escaped the modern ravages of pollution. It hasn't.

The project that most adversely and directly affected the lake was the channelizing, or straightening, in the late 1960s, of the Kissimmee River, a multi-million dollar project of the U.S. Army Engineers that turned a beautiful, meandering river into a 37-mile drainage ditch.

While it produced thousands of productive acres for ranchers and farmers, it also eliminated the pollution-filtering function nature had set up in the marshes. Even a lake the size of Okeechobee has a limit to the nutrient load it can handle. The lake water has

deteriorated in quality and probably will continue to do so.

In the late 1970s, a study was made to see if the fiasco could be undone by "dechannelizing" to some extent. The Engineers conceded the channel did hurt the lake—no small concession, since the lake is the source of drinking water for some three million Floridians. At this writing, no one has yet been seen building marshlands or rerouting water.

Lake Okeechobee experienced disastrous hurricane-driven floods in 1926 and 1928. In September of 1926, a major hurricane battered Miami and then crossed over to the lake. The wind-whipped waters overran and crumbled the crude muck dikes, then raged on to the community of Moore Haven on the western side of the lake. Between three and four hundred people were killed or injured. This occurred at the time people were still fighting over drainage and control of the lake, and which problem should come first.

Two years later, almost on the anniversary of the 1926 hurricane, another one zeroed in on Palm Beach, then headed for Lake Okeechobee. On its way it first laid waste to the vegetable farms, with Belle Glade taking the brunt of the blow. But there were heavy losses on over one-third of the lake shore, from Port Mayaca to Lake Harbor. When it was over, the estimated death total stood at 2,400.

There was no debate after that. Control of the lake would have to come first, drainage later. President-elect Herbert Hoover came to make a personal inspection. Federal aid was disbursed, and from there on it was a long, expensive, but absolutely necessary, job of harnessing the lake with dikes, levees, hurricane gates and all the other controls that engineering could provide.

Today, thousands cruise across or around the lake, many of them unaware of the twin disasters in the '20s, and perhaps equally unaware the fight still goes on over drainage that is so vital to special interests and much-abused nature.

The eastern end of the cross-state waterway from Port Mayaca to Stuart was not completed until 1937. It was officially opened on March 22, with a flotilla of yachts assembling at Stuart. A two-day cruise to Fort Myers was made with an overnight stop at Clewiston. Along the way, towns staged celebrations as the Gulf and the Atlantic were joined by a water route. The Stuart *News* reported that in the first 52 days, 3,000 craft used the new section of the waterway.

Prior to the Mayaca-Stuart linkage, canals not much larger than ditches ran from Lake Okeechobee to West Palm Beach, Fort Lauderdale and Miami. They were shallow and rocky in places, more of a monument to man's insistence and stubborness than effective waterways.

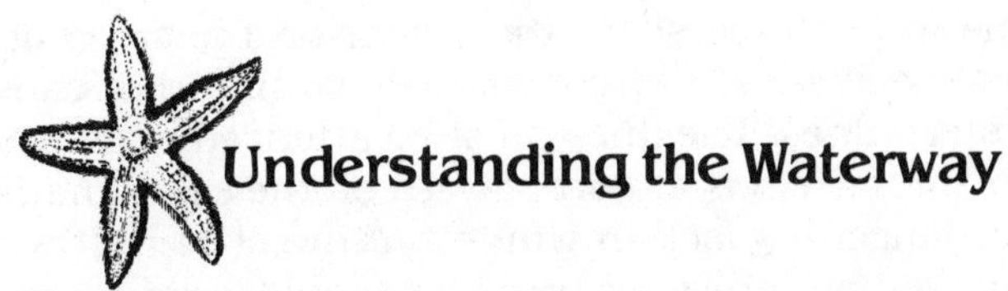

Understanding the Waterway

Two canals, two rivers, Lake Okeechobee and five locks comprise the basic Okeechobee Waterway. It is not complicated, despite its variety of components.

While passage through the locks is of concern to the first-timer, there is little need for apprehension. People who have cruised in other parts of the country where locks are common contend the lock operators and attendants along the Okeechobee are the most obliging.

"Locking-through" is simple here compared to some areas, where gunny sacks filled with straw and pike poles are part of the topsides defensive array. Nor is one thrown into the pit with large commercial craft, as is common in the New Orleans industrial lock or along the Gulf Intracoastal in Louisiana, where recreational craft are well down in the pecking order.

On the Okeechobee Waterway, 12 to 15 minutes is a normal "locking-through" time. Some of the old paper work has been eliminated. It's now down to only a couple of minutes of questions and answers. The lock equipment is good and if there are some less-than-pleasant attendants, we haven't met them.

The five locks, listed in east-to-west order, are St. Lucie, Port Mayaca, Moore Haven, Ortona and Franklin lock at Olga. The rise and fall at St. Lucie may range 10 to 15 feet, less at the others. West of the lake there are three locks that lower craft in easy stages.

The locks normally operate from 6 A.M. to 10 P.M., but in periods of drought the openings and closings might be restricted. It is permissible to lay over at any lock, though not within it. Dolphins, equipped with good-sized cleats, are convenient to tie up to. They are usually above or below the locks, sometimes both.

Ditch-running at night is more in the province of commercial boats. Pleasure boats usually find anchorages or make it to marinas before dark, but it is nice to know that in an emergency the dolphins are available and that fender systems outside locks can also be used.

Give two long and two short blasts when you first approach the lock area, though lock tenders will also understand if you are confused and blow the three-whistle signal used for drawbridges.

When preparing to enter a lock, it is advisable to lay well back until

the water within the lock is discharged; the turbulence is considerable. Wait for the water to go slack, then enter on the green light. Docking lines will be lowered to the boat crew so that they can arrange bow and stern lines. The lines must be attended at all times.

Newest lock in the system is at Port Mayaca on the east rim of the lake. It can be a dangerous lock in winds southwest to northwest. Engineering plans did not provide a breakwater or place of refuge for boats that might be stuck near the shore with the lock gates closed. The Corps of Engineers has recognized the problem but has not appropriated money, nor taken corrective action.

A call ahead on VHF Channel 16, while three or four miles from the lock, might be useful. Unless personnel are busy with lock traffic, you should get an answer right away. Your position report will give the lock operator some idea of your arrival time.

It's helpful to have the gate open or about to open. Even then, with wind astern, it can be a slippery entrance. Not many boat handlers we know care to see whitecaps in a lock. If the wind is out of the west and blowing even moderately, it is sometimes difficult for westbound, underpowered sailboats to get out of the lock. That's a problem that usually occurs in the winter months.

Under those conditions it may not be advisable to try a lake-crossing. Check the flag at the lock, ask if there is an anemometer reading available or seek an opinion from the lockmaster.

There are two routes to consider in navigating the lake—three, actually, if one wants to head for the Kissimmee River where there is a 14-foot vertical clearance restriction—and each has its supporters. They are known as Route 1 across the lake and the Rim Route. The Kissimmee Waterway off the lake enters at the northwest edge four miles below the town of Okeechobee.

From the Mayaca lock, a compass course for 15 miles can be set to Rocky Reef Light where a passage has to be made through a marked shoal area. Going east to Mayaca, a true course of 42 degrees will eventually line up with flashing strobe lights on the chimney stacks very near the entrance to the locks. Previously, the entrance had been difficult to find.

Don't try short cuts on the lake. Follow the charted course faithfully. The westerly crossing is completed at Clewiston, but finding the channel entrance can be difficult at times. A cylindrical structure is a clue to the general channel approach area.

In 1980, a lock was completed at Clewiston, replacing a hurricane gate. The lock may be kept in the open position when the lake level is 15.5 above mean sea level. Generally, the lake level adjustment is between 15.5 and 17.5 feet. In the hurricane season the level is dropped, a procedure that takes about 30 days for the discharge, a precautionary move that was learned in the hard lessons of the 1926 and 1928 hurricanes.

The Rim Route, longer by 12 miles, follows the east and south shores. It is the favorite with the more casual cruisers as well as some who don't want to be caught on the lake in any weather. On this route, all but 12 miles are protected by trees and islands. However, those 12 open miles in northwesterly weather mean being pinned uncomfortably close to a rocky lee shore.

In easterly winds, the Rim Route really pays off, for most of the run can be made under the protection of the land. At Clewiston, roughly the halfway point between Fort Myers and Stuart, the two routes join.

Westward to the Gulf

The Okeechobee Waterway is not having a good traffic year if fewer than 6,000 boats cross it. Figures show the peak months are December through April, and that far more westbound boats are being seen than formerly was the case.

Most of the Intracoastal Waterway travelers who come down from Norfolk continue on to the Florida Gold Coast, but an increasing number turn to starboard where the St. Lucie Inlet's west end intersects the ICW.

They cruise up the St. Lucie River unless a stop is scheduled for the always-popular Manatee Pocket harbor near Salerno, just below Stuart. That's often crowded in the winter months, so we more often set up our westward crossing by anchoring at Hog Cove, north of the Route A1A bridge and three miles up from the St. Lucie-ICW turnoff. We also use it when passing through to the east. It never seems to be crowded, the holding ground is good and, other than a little rocking from boats using the waterway, it's been satisfactory.

Another anchorage we have used is along the shore near Sewell Point. It is not always restful there because currents sweep around the point, and with an opposing wind it can get a little bumpy. On the other hand, it is a good place to pick up a cool breeze from the Atlantic, and the view is pleasant.

Our principal recollection of this anchorage concerns hull noises that were the loudest and most persistent we have encountered.

Marine life, riding the current, gather around the hull making crackling, snapping sounds. Nearly all newcomers to Florida cruising experience it sooner or later.

While tied up at Everglades City one day, the owner of a boat behind us tentatively knocked on *Final Edition's* hull and asked to speak to me. He seemed nervous and quickly got to the point. "I hear crackling and snapping sounds in the hull of my boat, just as though there were a fire. There's no smoke but I am concerned that perhaps a wire, or wires, are burning. Maybe some electrical connection is arcing."

We went to his boat and I immediately recognized the hull sounds. He and his wife accepted the marine life explanation with apparent relief.

As for that night in the St. Lucie River, when it seemed the local marine population was holding a corn-popping contest under our boat, Peggy also heard thumping and rapping sounds, almost loud enough to be startling, not unlike a dinghy bumping a hull. It seems there are fish in the porgy family that crack shells with grinding plates in their mouth. And shrimp can make clicking or crackling sounds.

What makes the sounds eventually go away? Our uneducated guess is that when tidal currents start to lose force, the noisemakers go off somewhere else to have a hull of a good time.

If the Okeechobee Waterway is unique in that it passes through the cow country core of south Florida, presenting still another view of the state, then the flavor and individuality of the communities along the way contribute strong supporting roles.

At the two ends, Stuart on the east, Fort Myers-Fort Myers Beach on the west, the ever-increasing population growth rates have reshaped the towns' original, apparent destinies of being mainly winter tourist communities propitiously positioned along the waterfront.

Fort Myers and its contiguous communities are exploding, and acknowledged as one of the fastest growing areas in the nation. People have come not to visit but to stay. This growth has also resulted in a whopping increase in boating interest. One of the chief reasons for living there is to take advantage of the Gulf, river and waterway delights.

Stuart, once a slow-paced town that attracted people of conservative tastes, and famed for its fresh and saltwater fishing, has experienced the common Florida malady known as growing pains. From the flying bridge, however, our view is that Stuart hasn't changed so drastically that it can not be recognized by those who passed by in boats 20 or more years ago.

It still is a pleasant place to visit, and its old charm is reflected along the waterfront in many places. Marine facilities are first-rate, and David Lowe's boatyard in nearby Port Salerno continues to be well known by veteran boat owners up and down the coast. From a passing boat, what is visible reflects well-groomed homes, interesting estates on high-crowned land to the northeast leading to Sewell Point, and the impression that the community has a style of its own.

The St. Lucie River's attractiveness is perhaps lost upon the transient who sees it solely as part of the Okeechobee Waterway, overlooking the river's own merits. The St. Lucie North Fork, for example, is popular with local and visiting boatmen. Going west, the Fork is to starboard, immediately after the U.S. 1 drawbridge at Stuart. There is a marina which is part of a resort complex, beyond Greenbridge Point, while the upper reaches of the North Fork rate mention for their good dinghy cruising and fishing waters.

Heading west, beyond Palm City on the Intracoastal near the St. Lucie lock, mangroves, palmettos and heavy underbrush line the channel sides, a clue that the coastal fringe is behind and the revealing trip across-state is really beginning.

Two miles west of the St. Lucie lock a bridge straddles the waterway only six feet above the surface. For several years it has been faithfully opened by a woman who lives in a small, neat home a few yards from the northeast end of the bridge.

After you have blown the whistle signal for opening the draw, don't expect her to come flying out of the house immediately. She tends to be involved in household tasks; but she'll get to the bridge as soon as she can, walking ladylike out to her task at the controls. As you guide your boat through, she will smile, nod her head and note the registration number and, if possible, the name of it.

It's 91 statute miles to the next lady tender of the draw, at Fort Denaud, east of Alva. She works out of a small white building and, as far as can be determined, she has no other duties that might distract her from the whistle signals of approaching boat traffic.

Women drawtenders may seem to some an example of the modern trend of equal work opportunity, regardless of sex, but, in Florida, at least, they've been around for many years. One, at Moore Haven, always seemed to be in the midst of hanging out a spectacularly long line of washing when we came along.

It was a common sight along the waterway, even as late as the 1950s and mid-60s, to see hand-operated drawbridges in some rural

areas. Josephine Campbell, drawbridge tender for nearly 40 years at the Blackburn Point Bridge on the ICW at Osprey, near Venice, knew something about that.

She had to open the bridge by picking up a 25-pound handle bar, inserting it into a metal slot, and pushing against it while walking several times in a circle. "Walking the bridge around," it was termed. Josephine probably developed the leg muscles of a football fullback.

She worked the night shift and got used to napping with "one ear open," ready to spring into action like a sleeping fireman waiting for the station alarm bell to sound. Josephine was a favorite with the tug operators pushing or towing barges in the night hours.

It was 1968 before Josephine Campbell could cease walking the bridge around. Electric controls were put in then, though she was instructed to keep the handle bar handy "just in case" the power went out.

A French Lady's Fiefdom

To many who cruise the Okeechobee Waterway, the marina at Indiantown is a friendly, well-run operation. Lying behind a cut between two high embankments, the marina's reputation as a natural "hurricane hole" was put to the test by Hurricane David in 1979. Even though David did not make a direct hit, winds did gust to 70 mph or so, and the boats came through without major trouble.

About a mile east of the marina, on a high rise of land just off the waterway, there is a small "stadium." It's not for football—it's the Indiantown Rodeo Bowl. Movie star and frustrated cowboy Burt Reynolds is one of its financial supporters. In Indiantown, among the young people, doing well in the annual high school rodeo outranks being a football hero. What really counts is what the boys and girls can do in bull riding, barebacking on broncos, wrestling steers, goat-tieing, calf roping and other forms of cow-country contesting.

You've cruised into the unnautical land of pointy-toed boots, cowboy hats and cattle range riders.

Some say that if you've seen the Rodeo Bowl, the marina, the local inn, the little shopping center and the junction of state roads 76 and 710, you've seen all there is to see in Indiantown. That doesn't take into account the bank or one of the friendliest post offices we've ever been in.

In the mirrored stillness of the Indiantown Marina on the Okeechobee Waterway, a version of a flat-bottomed, junk-rigged vessel, its pole masts, elevated poop and generous overhang reflected inversely in the water, is absorbed in the early morning light. Once described as "the marina in the meadow, complete with meadowlarks," the Indiantown Marina is about nine miles east of Lake Okeechobee.
Marston photo

This is the town basically "owned" by Yvonne Famel, of Paris, New York and Palm Beach. By stretching the word fiefdom a bit, it could be said she presided over our nation's only fiefdom as the decade of the 1980s opened.

Several years ago, she bought several acres of unincorporated Indiantown as a family investment, then formed a company to do some developing. To build the town, she established a bank, built water and sewer plants, constructed the marina, arranged for garbage disposal and other municipal services, including what amounts to a locally operated telephone system. Her Indiantown Company is efficient and so are the people who operate it for her. Everything works on schedule. You can count on it. The drinking water is claimed to be the best in the state. There's an industrial park and even a small steel mill on the outskirts of town. There's talk of expanding the marina as part of a larger development, even building a golf course, maybe a condominium or two, country-style.

The town's showplace is the Seminole Inn, built in 1925 by S. Davies Warfield, president of the Seaboard Railroad. He had it built as a hunting lodge as well as an inn for travelers coming to the end of the railroad line. When plans to make Indiantown a railroad center failed years ago, the inn's future became clouded. (Warfield was the uncle of Wallis Warfield, who married the Duke of Windsor. The Duke and Duchess spent part of their honeymoon at the Seminole Inn.)

The inn fell on hard times, but a few years ago it was restored. Today, a touch of the Old South grandeur exists in the lobby with its open fireplace and twin white staircases.

The Indiantown Marina is one of our favorites. Maybe because it's the only one we know that's built in a meadow and comes complete with meadowlarks. There is also a resident alligator, a freeloader with a weakness for marshmallows. (It's not wise—nor legal—to feed alligators; they might not know a marshmallow from a poodle that fell overboard.)

The resident 'gator is called Albert. He appeals to transient boatmen, but is regarded as a nuisance by some of those who live aboard boats in Indiantown. One year Albert surprisingly deposited a clutch of eggs in the grass at one end of the marina, thus causing his name to be changed to Albertina for a time.

Albert is the prime marina attraction despite the fact that Burt Reynolds keeps his houseboat, *Lucky Lady*, there. Burt never gets to use it, so there's little sense hanging around the marina, mouth agape and eyes bugged, to get a glimpse of The Great One. Chances for that are better when something big is going on at the Indiantown Rodeo Bowl.

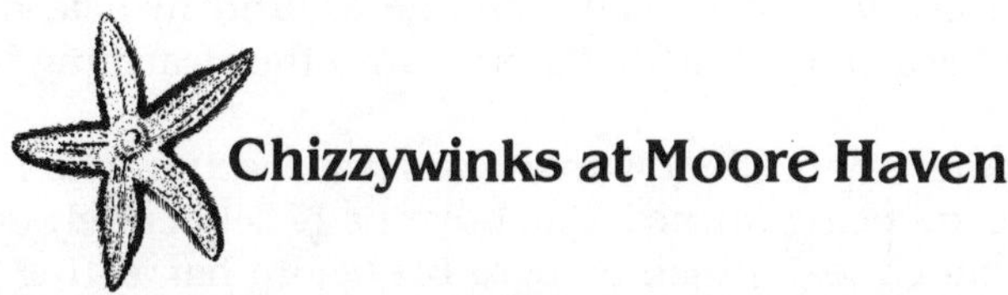

Chizzywinks at Moore Haven

There's something to first impressions being lasting ones. We first stopped at Moore Haven's town dock in December of 1952 and almost immediately saw our first real live cowboy gallop into town. They didn't have those in Boston where I had just come from.

What Peggy and I were looking at wasn't a western-type cowboy. It was a "Cracker Cowboy," a type of cowboy whom Frederic Remington, the well known cowboy artist and western authority in the 1890s, said "lacked dash and were indifferent riders." He did admit they were "picturesque in their unkempt, almost unearthly wildness."

They rarely used a rope, seldom a six-gun. Remington saw them as cattle hunters more than cowboys, wild-looking individuals with hanging hair and drooping hats. He was probably right but I take my first-time cowboys as I find them in Moore Haven.

The town dock is just west of the lock, a handy overnight place to be positioned for the 6 A.M. opening. Going west, the strategy is to get through the lock before dark and tie up at Moore Haven.

For years, the routine was to get settled down, plug into the electricity, top off the water tank and relax before dinner. Maybe the deputy sheriff would come to collect the dockage fee, maybe he wouldn't. On Friday and Saturday nights there sometimes were more important things for him to do.

Now there is a more businesslike arrangement. The dockage charge—the same for all size boats—is still modest, though increased. Take the money across the street and drop it into a metal box bolted to the cement floor of the small city hall lobby. And help yourself to a ready-made money receipt. Just sign your name.

Once, in the old days, when the deputy did come aboard, he quickly pushed the sliding door tight in *Final Edition*'s cabin. "Have to close up fast or the chizzywinks will mess things up. They leave little brown stains everywhere," he explained. And if they can't get in, they will cling to the cabin sides after dark when interior lights are on.

Chizzywink is the local name for an insect which looks like an overgrown mosquito. They are yellow-green in color, and hatch by the millions on Lake Okeechobee, especially along the Rim Route. For some unexplained reason, they swarm around the Australian pines at lakeside. When the wind is blowing through the pines, the

chizzywinks are blown into the water. That's when the bluegill fishing becomes crazy. The bluegills charge around in a feeding frenzy. Flyrod fishermen cast artificial bugs into the swarming fish. Everyone loads up.

A worse nuisance than Chizzywinks, however, occurs when the sugar cane fields are being burned. The burning is deliberately done to get rid of as much leafy trash as possible before harvesting the cane. It saves the sugar companies money in the harvesting and milling process but it does nothing for the betterment of humans outside the industry.

If the wind is from the wrong direction, a boat at the town dock—or anywhere along the waterway in the general vicinity—will be coated with the sooty ash from the fields. Author Phil Francis, who lived and worked in Clewiston for many years, says the burning trash removes 91 billion cubic feet of oxygen each year. He has further publicly charged it reduces rainfall by as much as 25 percent, and affects the lifestyle of every living creature in South Florida.

Chizzywinks and sooty ash notwithstanding, we still stop at Moore Haven. The nuisances take place only at certain periods of the year.

Moore Haven does have a burned-out look about it and one may wonder what things were like in its heyday. As a matter of fact, it was once a very lively place, named after James Moore, a native of Nova Scotia who made and lost fortunes in land operations in various parts of the United States.

In their book *Lake Okeechobee, Wellspring of the Everglades*, the husband and wife writing team of Alfred and Kathryn Hanna devote a whole chapter to the duchess of Moore Haven. The duchess was Marian Newhall Horwitz O'Brien, a Philadelphia socialite who moved to Moore Haven. Her first husband was George Quintard Horwitz, a prominent Philadelphia lawyer who invested in Moore Haven land with his friend, John J. O'Brien, former city editor of the Philadelphia *Public Ledger*. When he died suddenly, "the duchess" came to Moore Haven to oversee the property.

She stayed and soon proved to be a remarkably good businesswoman, a mover and doer. She also became one of the first woman mayors in the country. Later, she married O'Brien and as a team they cut a wide swath around the Lake Okeechobee farmlands.

The O'Briens did a lot for Moore Haven, but they did have their critics. Apparently, it went against the local grain to see them in riding breeches astride fancy horses. The O'Briens also annoyed the Moore Haven regulars when they attempted to establish a town named Newhall, north of Moore Haven. Several English families were persuaded to take up residence there, but their presence bothered the locals. People talked about the men drinking tea every afternoon and their wives smoking cigarettes in long holders. Newhall didn't last very long.

Then, when blacks moved into Moore Haven to provide labor for harvesting crops and railroad construction, white labor walked out. The O'Briens sided with the blacks and won in a two-day, tense showdown, but they became very unpopular thereafter with many of the residents.

Whether that caused them to move 26 miles southeast of Moore Haven, we do not know. They became interested in a colony of Japanese farmers there, and with characteristic enterprise, began to establish and promote a city we know today as Clewiston. They named it in honor of A.C. Clewis, an influential banker friend from Tampa.

Despite their good works, the O'Briens fell into disfavor once again. One night, a shot fired through the window of their house, missed John but nicked Mrs. O'Brien. Furious, she dropped her social aplomb and gentle bearing, grabbed a revolver and ran out into the night unsuccessfully trying to find the assailant.

The end came when their home was burned down and they lost everything. Eventually, the Duchess of Moore Haven moved to Palm Beach, then on to Detroit, where she died.

LaBelle of the Waterway

Henry Ford liked LaBelle. So did his close, inventive friends, Thomas Edison and Harvey Firestone. Ford was so taken with the town that he bought the Everett Hotel there in 1910. People first came by excursion boat, the only sensible way to travel in the early 1900s. Today, this small town on the Caloosahatchee River, 30 miles up from Fort Myers, still attracts people, who arrive by boat.

The three titans of industry came to LaBelle because Firestone was doing some experimental planting of goldenrod, which he hoped would lead to the manufacturing of synthetic rubber. Edison and Ford were also interested, Edison because he was searching for a cheap material to use for filament, Ford because he had ideas of buying some land.

The Ford venture was successful, but not those of Firestone and Edison. When the first crude road was built from Fort Myers to

LaBelle, Ford was one of the first to use it. Blitz Wegman, the local dealer who started selling Fords in 1926, tells of Ford driving in one day behind the wheel of a Lincoln, but with someone following in a Model T, the car he advertised as The Car That Will Take You There and Back.

LaBelle is small—population around 3,000—and friendly. There are about 175 cattle ranchers in Hendry County where LaBelle is the county seat. At one time, it had the highest per capita income in the state.

The little city is proud of its waterfront, with parks maintained on either side of the river. The town has always been hospitable to boating and cruising people. Although the town dock, about long enough for two 35-foot boats, was built back in the Works Progress Administration (WPA) days, there never has been a dockage charge; electricity is also free. The dock is the worse for wear but it is adequate, and if there were to be a change, the delightful informality and welcome might be lost. The guest time limit, however, is 72 hours, which is most generous.

A small, modern library is across the street from the dock, on the site of Ford's old Everett Hotel. The library welcomes cruising people and stocks a good bit of local history on the shelves.

The streets back from state road 80, which runs through the center of the community, are lined with huge live oaks, their branches festooned with air plants which belong to the orchid family. Right after Hurricane David, the streets were littered with scores of air plants.

For many years, the one place in town where transients and locals alike gathered regularly was Flora and Ella's restaurant, a combination Western Union office and coffee shop. Ella and Flora Burchard started the restaurant in 1935, and worked long hours from 5 A.M. to 9 P.M. daily over the years.

In 1979, one sister retired and moved out of town, and the remaining sister told me, "I'm plumb wore out and unless I quit real soon, there's going to be a big funeral in this town." It created a kind of crisis in LaBelle. Good food is good food but what about losing Ella and Flora? Last we heard, a search was on for a buyer, "just the right type" of person who wouldn't mess up the country cooking and famous pies the sisters turned out.

Normally, making a purchase of honey is a routine part of shopping, but not in LaBelle. Buying honey here, particularly after store hours, is on the honor system. There is a small cluster of honey stores on state road 80, about a six- or seven-minute walk from the dock.

One of the last "free" docks in Florida is at LaBelle on the Okeechobee Waterway. The dock dates from Depression days; it is a popular stop, as is the small, friendly community of LaBelle itself. Electricity and water are provided. The unwritten rule of free time: 72 hours.
Marston photo

After closing time, honey in various-sized containers, each with the price marked, is left on the shelves of the outer display room. Customers make their selections and the correct amount of money is put in a slot on the office wall. Proprietors tell us the system works beautifully and they don't expect it to be otherwise.

And then there is the story of the Warren family.

In the spring of 1949, Edward C. Warren steamed along the Caloosahatchee River in his 114-foot yacht, *Navette.* Aboard were his daughters, Marjorie and Dorothy, and a son, George. At LaBelle, immediately east of the town dock, Warren slowly maneuvered the big yacht into a lagoon, shut down the power and tied her up. She was never to cruise again. Today, *Navette* is still there, though the once-gleaming yacht is rotting away in shallow water close to shore.

Warren had bought a small island in the lagoon, which he planted with guava, papaya, hickory, banana trees, and about 100 coconut palms. Later he acquired goats and chickens. An income-producing trailer park was built; he had come to stay.

The *Navette* did not suddenly become a home for his family. It had, in fact, been a floating residence for several years, and had been cruised extensively. Mrs. Warren had lived aboard, too, but died prior to the LaBelle trip. The 114-footer, until 1938, had been owned by J.P. Morgan, who used it as a commuter yacht from Long Island to Wall Street.

Warren himself was a well known engineer, a scientist and a Florida land developer. It was unlikely LaBelle was just a chance stop while cruising.

The son, George, eventually moved ashore, but the spinster sisters have never left the boat.

Marjorie and Dorothy have always considered *Navette* to be "home." The old yacht is cluttered with mementoes of long ago. Prominently displayed in the main cabin is a picture of Mr. Warren, who died in 1960, still revered by his daughters. If it's possible to live on memories, the Warren sisters are doing it.

Many cruisers think the dozen or so miles between LaBelle and Alva are the most attractive on the entire Okeechobee Waterway. The waterway winds between rows of citrus groves, the foliage along its banks is green and lush. The soil has always been rich, the most fertile in the Caloosa Valley.

In the 1960s, the Corps of Engineers did some straightening out of the river above and below Alva, but not enough to remove the delights of cruising the Caloosahatchee. In the old days, the river route was so winding and twisting, that some of the riverboats bound to and from

Lake Okeechobee had to be warped around the tight turns.

A key place on the Waterway is Fort Myers, a city historically active on the waterfront. Its city yacht basin is the perfect layover stop. A main highway passes by the marina, and there is an active commercial airport.

It is a mailport and a good place to obtain marine supplies. The city dockmaster for many years, Captain Ed Hansen, is Florida's best-known in his field. He is also known for fighting potentially bad boating legislation in both Tallahassee and Washington.

There really is no equal of the 151-mile-long Okeechobee Waterway. There is only one LaBelle, one duchess of Moore Haven, one vital Lake Okeechobee and, for sure, only one town owned lock, stock and barrel by a woman from Paris.

THE EAST SIDE STORY

Chapter 14

Among the crusing clan's milestones, one memory common to all and long-remembered, occurs on the first trip south on the Intracoastal Waterway—that day when the boat crosses the St. Mary's River and enters Florida waters.

What is unique about that moment is that, alas, leaving Georgia and entering Florida is not like day unto night. In fact, Florida looks like Georgia and Georgia looks like Florida. Where are the palm trees, the sun-kissed beaches, the sparkling waters and what is that odor greeting us in such foul fashion? If this be Florida, how far is it to Fort Lauderdale?

The odor comes from the big pulp mill in Fernandina; and the distance to Fort Lauderdale is 348 statute miles. In that distance any initial disenchantment erodes as one moves along the ICW, the acronym which can also mean I-Can't-Wait to the more impatient Florida-bound.

Although some cruisers divide Florida's east coast into two large, but unequally distanced parts separated by the St. Lucie Inlet, I slice it differently. I think of Fernandina Beach through St. Augustine as the prime historical zone; Titusville through Melbourne-Eau Gallie as the space-age wonderland; Melbourne through Stuart as representative of Florida in another, less developed era, and Palm Beach to Miami as the Gold Coast.

The cruising Corinthian may view the southward-ho trek down the east coast as marginally appealing because it is restrictive and there is too much channel running. Indeed, some make a sizable portion of the trip on the outside, in the Atlantic. To others, however, cruising is moving along from one area to another, stopping to visit interesting places, seeing something as historic and old as St. Augustine and as new as the space center at Cape Canaveral. The pace is leisurely, but anticipation and excitement build as the gap closes each day on the ultimate objective—Miami.

It is not our intention to delineate city by city and marker by marker the 373 miles between Fernandina Beach and Miami. We leave that to the *Waterway Guide* and the *U.S. Coast Pilot.* Our intended mission is more general.

Peggy and I do not find the ICW on the Atlantic side confining, nor do we subscribe to the belief there is a paucity of anchorages. We would agree however, that the farther one goes south the more costly it is and the shorter—and more irritating—the distances between drawbridges become.

In 1513, that roving Spaniard Juan Ponce de León landed on Easter Sunday, March 27, and gave the land the name Pasqua

Florida (Feast of Flowers). Theories vary about where he landed—either Cape Canaveral or between St. Augustine and the St. Johns River. Ponce apparently found the Indians uniformly hostile, even shouting a few angry Spanish words which suggests that other landing parties, possibly slave hunters, may have preceded him.

Another foreign group landed on Florida shores as recently as 1942. On the morning of June 17, the German submarine U-584 surfaced at dawn not far offshore from Ponte Vedra Beach, a short distance south of Jacksonville Beach. Five men headed for shore in a small boat, four of them in bathing suits, all wearing German caps with the Nazi insignia.

Four of the men got out, loaded with heavy boxes full of dynamite, and buried them above the high tide line, only 200 feet or so from Florida State Road A1A. Buried with the boxes were the small shovels used for the hurried excavations. Some distance farther on, the men's caps were buried. These had been vital because, had the men been captured at the scene wearing the caps emblazoned with the swastika, they could have pleaded they were on a military mission. They would thereby have been subject to prisoner-of-war treatment, not the harsher fate that spies or saboteurs might expect.

One man rowed back to the submarine and the four others began to walk northward along the surf line, two playfully tossing a rubber ball back and forth. The other two carried duffle bags just large enough to contain changes of clothing. The U-boat slid beneath the surface of the Atlantic waters and the men, undetected as they changed clothes, left the beach, and later boarded a bus for Jacksonville where they went their separate, assigned ways.

Four days earlier, at Amagansett on New York's Long Island, four other Germans had landed. The grand plan was to blow up hydroelectric plants in New York, Tennessee and Illinois, Penn Station terminal in New York and a bridge over Hell Gate on the East River.

The sabotage plan was never carried out. One of the Amagansett group turned himself in to the FBI and soon the roundup was under way. Almost one year later, Nazi Edward John Kerling pointed out the Florida burial site to officials. The caps were also found.

Of the eight Germans tried by a military commission, six were given the death sentence; President Truman pardoned the other two after World War II ended. One of them, George Dash, wrote about the venture in his book, *Eight Spies Against America.* At Ponte Vedra Beach today, a modest-sized roadside marker calls attention to the landing of the Germans.

The Intracoastal south from Jacksonville Beach wends its way between the bluffs of the beachline to the east and the mainland, past broad and narrow bays; vigilance is required in keeping track of channel marker numbers.

The Best of ICW Cruising

It is possible to hoist sail and go cruising on the Intracoastal despite what you hear to the contrary. That there is good sailing is evidenced by the presence in Cocoa of the East Coast Cruising Association, one of the most active organizations of its kind in the state.

While it is true that on much of the ICW between Fernandina Beach and Miami you have to stick to the chummy confines of the established waterway, one notable exception is the 210-mile stretch from St. Augustine to Stuart. Within that distance, the Indian River runs for 120 miles and much of it can be sailed, with the right slant of wind.

Most southward-bound cruising boats begin their last leg to the Florida line in the vicinity of St. Simons Island, Georgia. The distance to Fernandina Beach is about 40 miles. Some anchor beyond Fernandina Beach but many pull into the famous old city to celebrate their arrival in Florida. Fernandina is even more interesting now because of a restoration program.

Florida's northernmost city should not be passed up by anyone remotely interested in history. It has been under eight flags since its discovery by French explorer Jean Ribault in 1562. Over the centuries, the city has come under the influence of Spanish conquistadors, French Huguenots, British loyalists, Yankee gunboats, Confederate blockade runners, and rum runners and hijackers. Fort Clinch, built in 1847 to protect the harbor, is located on Amelia Island, as is the city itself.

There is an anchorage area just west of the ICW opposite Fernandina Beach and other anchorages in Jackson and Kingsley creeks about three miles to the south. Ten to 15 miles farther there are anchorages just off the Intracoastal at the north end of Talbot Island, in Sawpit Creek and the Fort George River, all those within a five-mile segment of the ICW.

Twenty miles south of Fernandina, the St. Johns River crosses the

The last trace of a morning mist on the St. Johns River lies transparently just beyond a bend in the river, and reveals a lighted navigational aid in front of a feet-in-the-water cypress tree. And beyond, a first-class nautical outhouse, complete with stairway. Marston photo

ICW on the final five miles of its 276-mile course to the Atlantic. It is a real cruising bonus to leave the waterway and cruise up the St. Johns. The river can take you 150 miles, all the way to Sanford, or as short a distance as 14 miles, to the Jacksonville city waterfront. Another four takes you to the Ortega River area, the center of the city's marine industry and yacht services.

Many go on to Palatka, 40-odd miles south of Jacksonville. Over that stretch, the river is often two miles wide with high shores (by Florida standards) and heavily forested. Water is deep enough in most places to cruise close to shore.

Before Palatka, tidal influences will have dropped off, but the flow of the river will be a mild opposing force. The St. Johns River flows northward, one of three major rivers in North America that has that unique distinction. Beyond Palatka the river narrows and from there to Sanford, across lakes—one of them the 10-mile-long Lake George—and around bends, lies some of Florida's best and most intimate cruising. Many loyalists rate it above the more publicized coastal cruising grounds on either Florida coast.

We have found the little river towns pleasant places to stop and Sanford a good turnaround point. There are a few good restaurants and catfish lovers will find them a house specialty.

The 210-statute-mile distance between the junction of St. Johns River and the ICW and the St. Lucie Inlet farther south at Stuart is better studied if divided into two sections: Jacksonville Beach to Daytona Beach, and Daytona to Stuart. The first portion is a little over 70 miles, the next close to 135 miles.

Beach Marine at Jacksonville Beach has long been one of the key stops for ICW travelers. It is strategically located and the management is well-tuned to the needs of transients.

Between there and Daytona, the longtime favorites are St. Augustine and Marineland. For many years, St. Augustine had insufficient space for all who wanted to stop by boat and visit the city. Now, more marina space has opened north and south of St. Augustine's Bridge of Lions, which crosses the Intracoastal. Those who prefer to anchor may do so out from the city marina or in the San Sebastian River, where there is good protection. The historic background of the nation's oldest city needs no elaboration here.

Southbound yacht skippers should give some advance thought to crossing the St. Augustine Inlet. The current can be strong, the crossing rough in a blow out of the east; spring tides, of course, produce stronger currents. There is a vertical lift bridge just north of the inlet; thus, if you pass through with adverse conditions ahead, you are already committed, though the distance over the troublesome portion is not very long.

We recall coming southbound towards the inlet in nasty weather one afternoon and hearing, on the marine radio, pleas for guidance from a sailboat crew strange to the waters, trying to make it through the inlet under confusing conditions. A very knowledgeable boat captain in the Camachee Cove marina, just north of the inlet, talked the sailboat in by radio, almost as though he had the boat in view. Although we have never been in that relatively new and modern marina, Peggy and I were impressed with the concern and guidance demonstrated, and marked it down as a place to be remembered.

In view of its popularity, the problem at Marineland, 20 miles beyond St. Augustine, is enough space for transients. That space issue should be solved by now with the addition of a new marina at Palm Coast, a short distance from Marineland.

Daytona Beach is known for many features—its beaches, automobile racing history and as a resort area. But to those who cruise the Intracoastal Waterway, it is another of those too-few, has-everything places. In recent years, there has also been an increase in the sailboat population and enthusiasm, even to the extent of a Daytona-to-Bermuda race every other year.

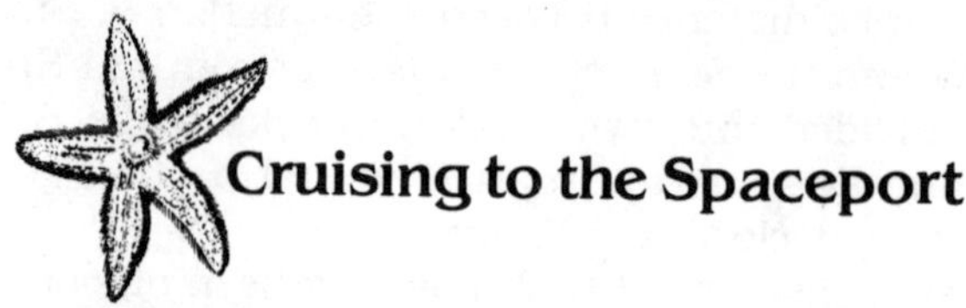

Cruising to the Spaceport

Few sights, it seems to us, observed from the cockpit or deck of a boat could surpass the thrill of seeing a manned spaceship thunder off from a launch pad on a mission that will take it 250,000 miles out from planet Earth.

Along with millions of other Americans, Peggy and I had watched the launches on television and had hoped that one day we could cruise into Spaceport. It took time, but we got there.

In the summer of 1979, Peggy and I took *Final Edition* into Spaceport waters for the first time. In our rather extensive cruising of Florida, it was, and is, one of the high points, although the restricted area from which we viewed the activity left us so far back from the massive structures, we still required binoculars to see anything reasonably close-up.

Actually, it was not necessary to crowd the fringes of the restricted areas. There were scores of anchorages along the ICW. One section of the waterway grandstand stretched from Titusville to Eau Gallie, a distance of 40 miles.

Still, it was exciting to wake up in our protected anchorage and take the morning's 360-degree look-around against the backdrop of assorted buildings, hangars and the Moonport, the world's largest building. In the better mood that breakfast can provide, the morning appraisal made me realize that we had simply made a side trip to a world-famous site, and it was worthwhile to have done so.

Today, the north 20 miles of the Space Center Area is the Canaveral National Seashore, the lands and waters again available to boatmen, fishermen and other nature lovers. The area had been closed to the public in the busier years of the National Aeronautics and Space Administration (NASA). A large wildlife refuge was kept undisturbed—a seeming contradiction in view of the NASA program. Wherever possible, however, a compatible balance was achieved. Existing orange and grapefruit groves were harvested in season and beekeepers went about their business of collecting honey. Ducks and shorebirds nested within sight of the launching pads, while wild pigs and other animals roamed among the scrub palmettos.

Yet the earth did tremble on Merritt Island and the stillness of the cape was shattered by noises most human ears had never heard before. The skies were flared at night and towers steamed like tea kettles. But owls in the refuge never blinked an eye, not even that day when the men from Merritt Island walked on the moon.

The most common approach to Spaceport is to turn off the ICW just north of the City Point bridge, at mile 894, the listed distance from Norfolk. The Cape Canaveral Barge Canal, three miles long, leads to the Banana River where a turn north permits up to seven miles of cruising along a well-marked channel until the restricted area boundary is reached.

It is possible to stay on the barge canal route, go through a lock and enter Port Canaveral. Another approach is to come in off the Atlantic through the jettied entrance four miles southwest of Cape Canaveral Light. The entrance is well buoyed and maintained, and used by local fishermen, shrimpers, tankers and recreational craft. There are also facilities for transient pleasure craft.

Our access was by still another way. We knew from studying the chart and local knowledge that it was possible to leave Melbourne and use the Banana River northward to the Spaceport. It would involve, however, getting by two or three shallow places.

We did have to creep around some channel bends and watch for unmarked shoals but by going slowly we were able to pick our way through the touch-and-go areas. It is not the route for those in a hurry, nor for sail or powered craft that don't fit under the two 36-foot-clearance Banana River bridges. The Intracoastal better suits the requirements of deeper draft boats and those adhering to a time schedule.

Practically, the best way to really visit the Spaceport region is to take a bus tour. Buses leave regularly from Titusville, Cocoa, Eau Gallie and Melbourne. The marinas have schedule information. Among the things to see are the Moonport, Astronaut Training Center, Merritt Island Visitor Center, Rocket Museum, the Apollo movies, launching pad and spaceship.

New Smyrna and South

To the crew aboard *Final Edition*, one of the most attractive portions of the entire Florida east coast lies between New Smyrna Beach and Vero Beach, all of it in the Indian River except for the north 23 miles. Much of the 23 miles is in Mosquito Lagoon, but the lagoon is wide and the ICW route gun-barrels down the west side. Don't overlook however, some of the six- and seven-foot places off the channel to the east that could suffice for emergency stops, overnight anchoring or dinghy trips over to the strip of land along the Atlantic.

The Indian River starts just south of the narrow, mile-long Haulover Canal, and continues all the way to the St. Lucie Inlet. Some fine sailing lies ahead if the wind direction favors, as it often does during the spring and fall.

On the small craft charts note the many places where the blue-colored areas, indicating shallow waters, give way to those of white, signifying deeper water. Be aware, too, after leaving Haulover and approaching Titusville, of the spoil bank "islands," around most of which are good anchoring depths and afford a measure of protection. From Titusville on, the dinghy can be towed for off-the-waterway stops and short trips to the islands.

Marinas exist all along the way, most of them more functional than flashy. Melbourne-Eau Gallie is particularly blessed in that respect, with good marinas on both sides of the ICW.

For us, not to stop at the Eau Gallie Yacht Basin, 74 nautical miles south of Daytona Beach, 150 miles north of Miami, would be to miss one of the highlights of an east coast cruise. It is a feeling not exclusive to us, since we have seen the big guest register many times, filled with complimentary remarks. Many of them are repeat expressions from old-timers, who like to see white-painted wooden buildings, roomy boat sheds and shade trees around the boatyard, happy that the warmth has not given way to plastic and sharp edges. A covered wet storage basin holds more than 40 boats, there are two marine railways and a building for engine work; a small, covered area called Ye Yachtsman's Old Work Shoppe displays a sign, "Please Use It."

Vero Beach is also highly regarded by most of the ICW migratory fleet. Going south, the charm begins 10 or so miles before reaching

Vero, where the waterway weaves through small wooded islands, past citrus groves, farms and the Pelican Island National Wildlife Refuge. Pelican Island, largest in the refuge, was established as such by President Teddy Roosevelt in 1903 and became Florida's first bird refuge.

Another landmark, north of Vero, is a long wooden dock off the waterway near Wabasso where, for years, yachts have stopped to buy grapefruit and oranges. A small fee is charged to those who wish to stop overnight.

Most cruising skippers prefer the option of a good anchorage or putting in at a good, well-equipped marina with a docking arrangement that does not remind one of an Olympic obstacle course. At Vero Beach, the ideal combination exists: good marinas and a protected anchorage within short rowing distance of the marine facilities. This delightful doubleheader is located on the north side of the Vero drawbridge. Only old-timers may know it, but the anchorage is in a section of the old ICW route.

On to the Gold Coast

The Gold Coast is a spectacular jolt to the cruising psyche if one takes cruising to mean a genteel, leisurely, away-from-it-all sort of thing. To hundreds of other transient yachtmen, especially in the winter months, it is a marine mecca for the faithful who have worked their way down from Norfolk on the ICW.

The Gold Coast has no geographical boundaries, though we think of it as the 70 miles between Lake Worth Inlet, just above Palm Beach, to downtown Miami's waterfront. Others make it 100 miles long, starting with St. Lucie Inlet.

That would include Hobe Sound, eight miles south of St. Lucie, which is related to the Gold Coast only in terms of affluence. The Jupiter Island lifestyle is one of exclusivity and conservatism that probably exceeds that of Palm Beach. The island is on the east side of Hobe Sound and on it is a 300-home, incorporated community lived in by wealthy, publicity-avoiding people who long ago staked out the island as their private residential preserve. Today, more than ever, they guard it fiercely.

What you see when cruising along the narrow confines of the ICW on Hobe Sound is a succession of lovely homes, meticulously

landscaped, shaded and surrounded by indigenous tropical flora. The houses, some occupied only in the winter months, were probably not meant to be "show places," at least in the Newport, Rhode Island, sense of the term. They were built with "old money values" for family use down through the generations.

Those who take the time may see shingled New England clapboard mansions or residences reflective of another era. The homes are fronted by long, royal-palm-lined driveways. Generous sweeps of closely trimmed lawn slope down to the water's edge. The high-rises, the condominia of the Gold Coast farther down the line, are not for Hobe Sound and the Jupiter Islanders. One island observer told feature writer Peter Gallagher, of the St. Petersburg *Times*, "These people are much older, more elegant, more conservative than those at Palm Beach. There's a 'true call,' here, none of that renting of shabby places as they do in Palm Beach."

The waters of Hobe Sound, however, are not off-limits to anyone. On the west side of the ICW channel there are three or four good places to anchor. We have enjoyed anchoring in the Sound and the surroundings, never more so than the early morning we raised anchor and cruised slowly past four or five manatees whose outlines were clearly defined in the clear water.

It's an eye-filling 70 miles from Lake Worth-Palm Beach on, so much so that anyone, let alone a hard-core Communist gazing upon mile after mile of gleaming yachts, beautiful estates and towering residential structures, might view it as a vulgar display of capitalism.

Seen from the Atlantic, the Gold Coast is comprised largely of a concrete coastline that goes on for miles and miles, wall-to-wall, with high-rise communal living and life on the grand vertical scale. The only clue to community identification generally is a blue, bulb-topped water tower that stands in some clearing to advertise, in bold letters, its civic existence.

On the Intracoastal side, the wide-eyed boatman, viewing for the first time what lies in the architectural wilds between Delray Beach and Miami, is properly awe-stricken while cruising along what we choose to call the Condominia Grand Canyon. This canyon has hundreds of windows inset in the canyon walls, and at each communal level, duplicate terraces. Dwellers occasionally appear in their assigned niches of the balcony empire to gaze down upon the ragged ranks of gawking cruising crews.

There are more than 1.4 million condominium residents in Florida. The largest concentration—a half million or so—is on the Gold Coast. In this unreal world of close condominium encounters, it is the one place where a yachtsman conceivably could be hit on the

Miami Beach is very much a part of cruising Florida. In the Florida Gold Coast areas, where high-rise apartment buildings line both sides of the Intracoastal Waterway, veteran cruising skippers refer to it as "Grand Canyon condominia cruising." Florida Division of Tourism photo

head with a falling geranium, complete with pot. The first hard-hat helmsman will appear somewhere south of Delray Beach.

The canyon, of course, is only a part, albeit a substantial part, of the Gold Coast. Modest homes as well as estates of considerable substance are seen close at hand. In some places, the ICW runs narrowly between seawalls, producing a chop and slop difficult to cope with at speeds barely above the steerageway control. To run faster is to curl a wake over the wall, across a swath of lawn and onto someone's patio. Seawall cruising requires piloting art, guidance on which is not to be found in the Rules of the Road.

Lunacy is both practiced and apparently permissible about six miles southward from Pompano Beach, in an Intracoastal Waterway zone we think of as Zanyville-by-the-Sea. It has been the misfortune of many to be caught in that area after school hours, in the crossfire of teen-agers playing "chicken" with high-powered outboard or stern-drive rigs. If the boats can't get up to 45 or 50 mph five seconds after a standing start, the kids probably won't set foot in them. The

more skilled of these rascals use your boat as a moving block that springs the aggressor speedboat free as soon as it cuts tight at full speed around the bow or stern. The frantic throttling of the roaring engines, the screams of propellers cavitating through a wall of thin water make one appreciate the quietude of the diving bell. The cacophony of the chicken quest rarely catches the ear of the waterway gendarmes, who always seem to be somewhere else looking for some boat operator going 200 rpms over the 6 mph limit. A session in Zanyville-by-the-Sea at least prepares one for dodging coconuts that have fallen into the waterway and bob around looking like so many mummified heads.

The Big Three on the Gold Coast comprise Palm Beach, Fort Lauderdale and Miami, three places really not alike in many respects, each with a style of its own, yet as a whole unlike anything else of its composite kind along the Atlantic, perhaps in the nation.

Fort Lauderdale is the pivot for the other two, an incredible waterfront city, only a small portion of which the average ICW traveler gets to see. Fort Lauderdale is still largely a working city with a sizable population of the newly rich, many of whom live in the canal colony in which yacht docklines are figuratively secured to brass doorknobs.

Palm Beach is the stronghold of the old aristocracy, and the winter home of the highly visible jet-setters.

Miami, ever-growing, continually takes pulse and stock of itself, seeking to determine if it is the new Havana or keeping pace on its own as the largest, best-known city in Florida, the gateway to South America and the southernmost home port of all the dreamboat society.

Landsat, the spacecraft, sees all of Florida in a satellite sweep of 111 seconds; our journey in this book, while of no such lofty purview nor comparable swift discernment, convinces Peggy and me all the more that no state is as blessed in cruising range and potential enjoyment.

It has strengths, it has weaknesses, it has variety, but in its 1,350 miles of coastline, plus its waterways and rivers, Florida presents a classic cruising cornucopia.

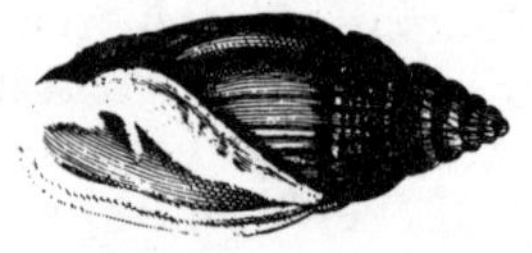

BIBLIOGRAPHY

Barnes, Bill. "Islandia, A Monument To Outdoor Sports." *Florida Sportsman.* Miami: Aug.-Sept. 1972.

Bishop, Barry C. "Landsat Looks at Hometown Earth." *National Geographic,* July 1976.

Dunn, Gordon E. and Miller, Banner I. *Atlantic Hurricanes.* Baton Rouge: Louisiana State University Press, 1964.

Earl, John. *John Muir's Longest Walk.* New York: Doubleday & Co. Inc., 1975.

Emmanuel, Michel G. *Tarpon Springs Sketch Book.* Tampa: Book One Ltd., 1974.

Hanna, Alfred and Kathryn A. *Lake Okeechobee, Wellspring of the Everglades.* New York: Bobbs-Merrill, 1948.

Lane, Carl D. *Go South Inside.* Camden, Maine: International Marine Publishing Co., 1977.

Lyons, Ernest. *My Florida.* New York: A.S. Barnes & Co., 1969.

Marth, Del and Martha J. *The 1978 Florida Almanac.* St. Petersburg: Willow Creek.

O'Reilly, John. *Boater's Guide to the Upper Florida Keys.* Coral Gables: University of Miami Press, 1970.

Papy, Capt. Frank. *Cruising Guide to the Florida Keys.* Minneapolis: Publication Arts, Inc., 1977.

Porter, Louise M. *The Chronological History of the Lives of St. Joseph.* Chattanooga: Great American Publishing Co., 1975.

Roscoe, Robert S. and Fessenden S. Blanchard. *A Cruising Guide to the Southern Coast.* New York: Dodd, Mead & Co., 1974.

Scherman, Katherine. *Two Islands.* Boston: Little, Brown & Co., 1971.

Smith, F.G. Walton. *The Seas in Motion.* New York: Thomas Y. Crowell Co., 1973.

Stevenson, George B. *Key Guide.* Tavernier, Florida: 1970.

Tannehill, Ivan Ray. *Hurricanes.* Princeton: Princeton University Press, 1943.

Tebeau, Charlton W. *A History of Florida.* Coral Gables: University of Miami Press, 1971.

———.*Man in the Everglades.* Coral Gables: University of Miami Press, 1968.

———.*The Story of the Chokoloskee Bay Country.* Coral Gables: University of Miami Press, 1955.

Truesdell, William G. *A Guide to the Wilderness Waterway.* Coral Gables: University of Miami Press, 1969.

United States Coast Pilots No. 4 & 5. Washington, D.C.

Waterway Guide, Southern Edition. Annapolis: 1980.

West, G.M. *Old St. Joe.* Pamphlet, 1922.

Will, Lawrence E. *Okeechobee Boats and Skippers.* St. Petersburg: Great Outdoors Publishing Co., 1965.

INDEX

O

P

R

S